THE ALEXANDER SHAKESPEARE

Romeo And Juliet

Edited by

R. E. S. YOUNGS

and

P de STE. CROIX

PREFATORY NOTE

This series of Shakespeare's plays uses the full Alexander text which is recommended by many Examining Boards. By keeping in mind the fact that the language has changed considerably in four hundred years, as have customs, jokes, and stage conventions, the editors have aimed at helping the modern reader – which English is his mother tongue or not – to grasp the full significance of these plays. The Notes, intended primarily for examination candidates, are presented in a simple, direct style. The needs of those unfamiliar with British culture have been specially considered.

Since quiet study of the printed word is unlikely to bring fully to life plays that were written directly for the public theatre, attention has been drawn to dramatic effects which are important in performance. The editors see Shakespeare's plays as living works of art which can be enjoyed today on stage, film and television in many parts of the world.

First edition 1972
Second edition 1983
Reprinted 1984, 1986, 1988, 1990, 1991, 1992, 1993

© HarperCollins Publishers

ISBN 0 00 325245 0

Published by Collins Educational
An imprint of HarperCollins*Publishers*
77–85 Fulham Palace Road, London W6 8JB

Made and printed in Great Britain by
HarperCollins Manufacturing, Glasgow

Contents

THE THEATRE IN SHAKESPEARE'S DAY

On the face of it, the conditions in the Elizabethan theatre were not such as to encourage great writers. The public playhouse itself was not very different from an ordinary inn-yard; it was open to the weather; among the spectators there were often louts, pickpockets and prostitutes; some of the actors played up to the rowdy elements in the audience by inserting their own jokes into the authors' lines, while others spoke their words loudly but unfeelingly; the presentation was often rough and noisy, with fireworks to represent storms and battles, and a table and a few chairs to represent a tavern; there were no actresses, so boys took the parts of women, even such subtle and mature ones as Cleopatra and Lady Macbeth; there was rarely any scenery at all in the modern sense. In fact, a quick inspection of the English theatre in the reign of Elizabeth I by a time-traveller from the twentieth century might well produce only one positive reaction: the costumes were often elaborate and beautiful.

Shakespeare himself makes frequent comments in his plays about the limitations of the playhouse and the actors of his time, often apologizing for them. At the beginning of *Henry V* the Prologue refers to the stage as 'this unworthy scaffold' and to the theatre building (the Globe, probably) as 'this wooden O', and emphasizes the urgent need for imagination in making up for all the deficiencies of presentation. In introducing Act IV the Chorus goes so far as to say:

> '. . . we shall much disgrace
> With four or five most vile and ragged foils,
> Right ill-dispos'd in brawl ridiculous,
> The name of Agincourt.'   (lines 49–52)

In *A Midsummer Night's Dream* (Act V, Scene i) he seems to dismiss actors with the words:

> 'The best in this kind are but shadows.'

4

Yet Elizabeth's theatre, with all its faults, stimulated dramatists to a variety of achievement that has never been equalled and, in Shakespeare, produced one of the greatest writers in history. In spite of all his grumbles he seems to have been fascinated by the challenge that it presented him with. It is necessary to re-examine his theatre carefully in order to understand how he was able to achieve so much with the materials he chose to use. What sort of place was the Elizabethan playhouse in reality? What sort of people were these criticized actors? And what sort of audiences gave them their living?

The Development of the Theatre
up to Shakespeare's Time

For centuries in England noblemen had employed groups of skilled people to entertain them when required. Under Tudor rule, as England became more secure and united, actors such as these were given more freedom, and they often performed in public, while still acknowledging their 'overlords' (in the 1570s, for example, when Shakespeare was still a schoolboy at Stratford, one famous company was called 'Lord Leicester's Men'). London was rapidly becoming larger and more important in the second half of the sixteenth century, and many of the companies of actors took the opportunities offered to establish themselves at inns on the main roads leading to the City (for example, the Boar's Head in Whitechapel and the Tabard in Southwark) or in the City itself. These groups of actors would come to an agreement with the inn-keeper which would give them the use of the yard for their performances after people had eaten and drunk well in the middle of the day. Before long, some inns were taken over completely by companies of players and thus became the first public theatres. In 1574 the officials of the City of London issued an order which shows clearly that these theatres were both popular and also offensive to some respectable people, because the order complains about 'the inordinate haunting of great multitudes of people, specially youth, to plays, interludes and shows; namely occasion of frays and quarrels, evil practices

5

of incontinency in great inns . . .' There is evidence that, on public holidays, the theatres on the banks of the Thames were crowded with noisy apprentices and tradesmen, but it would be wrong to think that audiences were always undiscriminating and loud-mouthed. In spite of the disapproval of Puritans and the more staid members of society, by the 1590s, when Shakespeare's plays were beginning to be performed, audiences consisted of a good cross-section of English society, nobility as well as workers, intellectuals as well as simple people out for a laugh; also (and in this respect English theatres were unique in Europe), it was quite normal for respectable women to attend plays. So Shakespeare had to write plays which would appeal to people of widely different kinds. He had to provide 'something for everyone' but at the same time to take care to unify the material so that it would not seem to fall into separate pieces as they watched it. A speech like that of the drunken porter in *Macbeth* could provide the 'groundlings' with a belly-laugh, but also held a deeper significance for those who could appreciate it. The audience he wrote for was one of a number of apparent drawbacks which Shakespeare was able to turn to his and our advantage.

SHAKESPEARE'S LIFE AND TIMES

Very little indeed is known about Shakespeare's private life: the facts included here are almost the only indisputable ones. The dates of Shakespeare's plays are those on which they were first produced.

*　　*　　*

1558 Queen Elizabeth crowned.
1561 Francis Bacon born.
1564 Christopher Marlowe born.

William Shakespeare born, April 23rd, baptized April 26th.

1566

Shakespeare's brother, Gilbert, born.

1567 Mary, Queen of Scots, deposed.
James VI (later James I of England) crowned King of Scotland.
1572 Ben Jonson born.
Lord Leicester's Company (of players) licensed; later called Lord Strange's, then the Lord Chamberlain's, and finally (under James) The King's Men.
1573 John Donne born.
1574 The Common Council of London directs that all plays and playhouses in London must be licensed.
1576 James Burbage builds the first public playhouse, The Theatre, at Shoreditch, outside the walls of the City.
1577 Francis Drake begins his voyage round the world (completed 1580).
Holinshed's *Chronicles of England, Scotland and Ireland* published (which Shakespeare later used extensively).
1582

Shakespeare married to Anne Hathaway.

7

1583 The Queen's Company founded by royal warrant.

Shakespeare's daughter, Susanna, born.

1585

Shakespeare's twins, Hamnet and Judith, born.

1586 Sir Philip Sidney, the Elizabethan ideal 'Christian knight', poet, patron, soldier, killed at Zutphen in the Low Countries.

1587 Mary, Queen of Scots, beheaded.
Marlowe's *Tamburlaine* (*Part I*) first staged.

1588 Defeat of the Spanish Armada.
Marlowe's *Tamburlaine* (*Part II*) first staged.

1589 Marlowe's *Jew of Malta* and Kyd's *Spanish Tragedy* (a 'revenge tragedy' and one of the most popular plays of Elizabethan times).

1590 Spenser's *Faerie Queene* (Books I-III) published.

1592 Marlowe's *Doctor Faustus* and *Edward II* first staged. Witchcraft trials in Scotland.
Robert Greene, a rival playwright, refers to Shakespeare as 'an upstart crow' and 'the only Shake-scene in a country'.

Titus Andronicus
Henry VI, Parts I, II and III
Richard III

1593 London theatres closed by the plague.
Christopher Marlowe killed in a Deptford tavern.

Two Gentlemen of Verona
Comedy of Errors
The Taming of the Shrew
Love's Labour's Lost

1594 Shakespeare's company becomes The Lord Chamberlain's Men.

Romeo and Juliet

1595 Raleigh's first expedition to Guiana. Last expedition of Drake and Hawkins (both died).

Richard II
A Midsummer Night's Dream

1596	Spenser's *Faerie Queene* (Books IV-VI) published. James Burbage buys rooms at Blackfriars and begins to convert them into a theatre.	*King John* *The Merchant of Venice* Shakespeare's son Hamnet dies. Shakespeare's father is granted a coat of arms.
1597	James Burbage dies; his son Richard, a famous actor, turns the Blackfriars Theatre into a private playhouse.	*Henry IV (Part I)* Shakespeare buys and redecorates New Place at Stratford.
1598	Death of Philip II of Spain.	*Henry IV (Part II)* *Much Ado About Nothing*
1599	Death of Edmund Spenser. The Globe Theatre completed at Bankside by Richard and Cuthbert Burbage.	*Henry V* *Julius Caesar* *As You Like It*
1600	Fortune Theatre built at Cripplegate. East India Company founded for the extension of English trade and influence in the East. The Children of the Chapel begin to use the hall at Blackfriars.	*Merry Wives of Windsor* *Troilus and Cressida*
1601		*Hamlet* *Twelfth Night*
1602	Sir Thomas Bodley's library opened at Oxford.	
1603	Death of Queen Elizabeth. James I comes to the throne. Shakespeare's company becomes The King's Men. Raleigh tried, condemned and sent to the Tower.	
1604	Treaty of peace with Spain.	*Measure for Measure* *Othello* *All's Well that Ends Well*
1605	The Gunpowder Plot: an attempt by a group of Catholics to blow up the Houses of Parliament.	
1606	Guy Fawkes and other plotters executed.	*Macbeth* *King Lear*

9

1607 Virginia, in America, colonized.
A great frost in England.

Antony and Cleopatra
Timon of Athens
Coriolanus
Shakespeare's daughter, Susanna, married to Dr. John Hall.

1608 The company of the Children of the Chapel Royal (who had performed at Blackfriars for ten years) is disbanded.
John Milton born.
Notorious pirates executed in London.

Richard Burbage leases the Blackfriars Theatre to six of his fellow actors, including Shakespeare.
Pericles, Prince of Tyre

1609

Shakespeare's *Sonnets* published.

1610 A great drought in England.

Cymbeline

1611 Chapman completes his great translation of the *Iliad*, the story of Troy.
Authorized Version of the Bible published.

A Winter's Tale
The Tempest

1612 Webster's *The White Devil* first staged.

Shakespeare's brother, Gilbert, dies.

1613 Globe Theatre burnt down during a performance of *Henry VIII* (the firing of small cannon set fire to the thatched roof).
Webster's *Duchess of Malfi* first staged.

Henry VIII
Two Noble Kinsmen
Shakespeare buys a house at Blackfriars.

1614 Globe Theatre rebuilt 'in far finer manner than before'.

1616 Ben Jonson publishes his plays in one volume.
Raleigh released from the Tower in order to prepare an expedition to the gold mines of Guiana.

Shakespeare's daughter, Judith, marries Thomas Quiney.
Death of Shakespeare on his birthday, April 23rd.

1618 Raleigh returns to England and is executed on the charge for which he was imprisoned in 1603.

1623 Publication of the Folio edition of Shakespeare's plays.

Death of Anne Shakespeare (née Hathaway).

10

INTRODUCTION

Romeo and Juliet holds many attractions for a young audience, not least its simplicity of design. The action is straightforward, undiverted by sub-plots and minor themes, and this is achieved through its concentration on the two lovers who gather the play into a unity. All the characters contribute to the main action and push it towards its conclusion. This unelaborate quality of the play is reinforced by the tightness of the time-scheme – the drama spans only five days in mid-July. The compression of the action binds the structure closely and indicates the kind of simplicity it achieves. But this is not to say that the play lacks variety; on the contrary, it is full of movement, colour and vigour, and it is given life by the gallery of individually realised characters.

The Language of the Play

The modern reader will face certain difficulties in *Romeo and Juliet*. These difficulties consist not so much in the strangeness of the words or the structure of the sentences, as in grasping quickly the purposes for which the language is used as it is. The Elizabethans (as those who lived during the reign of Elizabeth I are called) were as adventurous in their use of words as they were physically. Shakespeare too, delighted in playing about with words. He aimed to delight his audience by clever manipulation of the language. The pun is used often throughout this play. To the Elizabethans the pun was a perfectly legitimate device for the expression of deep emotion. Our own use of the pun today is rather different. The Elizabethan audience liked to hear ordinary events described in elaborate and dignified language; when Benvolio speaks of getting up before sunrise he says:

> *... an hour before the worshipped sun*
> *Peered forth the golden window of the east.*

11

A third feature of the language of the play is its open bawdiness – it is full of verbal jokes about sex. Two of the play's liveliest characters, Mercutio and the Nurse, are scarcely on stage without making bawdy remarks. Mercutio favours the double meaning – his remarks *could* be taken to be quite innocent. The Nurse is quite simply coarse. Here we find the essential contrast to the freshness, purity and frankness of the lovers' sexuality, a very special quality of their love.

Characterization

The names Romeo and Juliet have come to epitomize passionate young love, so successful was Shakespeare in creating these characters, through the power of poetry. They are quite different from each other. Romeo, seen first, is presented as the figure ever-present in Elizabethan poetry – a young man indulging himself in misery because he is rejected by the girl with whom he supposes himself in love. Through the elaborate and self-conscious words he speaks, we can gather that he has no real depth of feeling. His language becomes simpler and less artificial with the first words spoken to Juliet, though it is still somewhat contrived. Romeo, though young, is shown as a man of the world. But Juliet up to this point is presented as totally without emotional experience, imaginary or real. Told that she has a suitor, she says, in effect, that she will follow her mother's instructions. After the meeting with Romeo, however, she is transformed by the first arousal of her emotions, and in the balcony scene the two young people discover their true feelings. Romeo, released from playing with words about love, and Juliet, finding for the first time the world of sexual feeling, both speak directly to each other from the heart.

Following this scene, differences between the two become apparent again. Love, pure but sexually impassioned, is given superb expression in Juliet's soliloquy in Act II, Scene ii, and we are deeply struck by her emotional maturity. Romeo, caught up in the world of brawls and banishment, loses balance and becomes hysterical – he seems well short of heroic, though we do suffer for him

12

when we see his condition momentarily through the Nurse's eyes: 'Ah, sir! Ah, sir. Well, death's the end of all' (Act III, Scene iii, line 92). Juliet bears her troubles more steadily, and with clear determination. Finally Romeo, when his mind is also resolved, speaks lines over what he supposes is Juliet's dead body, which raise him to the rare dignity of a tragic hero. The boy we met dies a man, and a few moments later the girl we met dies a woman. It is this process of growth that makes their characterization so masterly, and so justly famous.

Though Shakespeare spends more time on the characterization of the two young lovers than upon anyone else, the play has a number of other parts of great interest. One of these is Mercutio: witty, high-spirited and courageous, he can easily dominate the first half of the play. His wit finds expression in a bewildering dexterity with words, which entertained the Elizabethan audience by being full of sexual overtone. Though Shakespeare gives him this abundant sexuality, it is important for the interplay between the characters that he has evidently never been in love, and indeed scarcely seems able to understand that emotion – 'he jests at scars who never felt a wound' (Act II, Scene ii, line 1). Though nominally Italian, Mercutio is given the qualities of a young Elizabethan Englishman – note his scorn for 'strange flies', these 'fashion-mongers' who affect continental manners. It is because of his irritation at Tybalt, whom he sees as just such a person, that he meets his death. His removal from the scene, though its immediate cause is an accident, is therefore a direct result of his character.

Tybalt, though more slightly drawn, is still a convincing person. With him, high spirits become contemptuous bravado and a sense of family honour an overbearing arrogance, which is rebuked even by the head of the family himself. This portrait is made a little more attractive by the fact that Juliet and the Nurse both loved Tybalt. Shakespeare knows well that characterization may be enriched by letting the audience see a person through the eyes of others as well as through their own.

Playing Benvolio might strike an actor as being less

exciting than portraying the other young men, but the skill shown in creating him is of the same order as in those other characters. Shakespeare needed someone against whom the extremes of Romeo and the fire and brilliance of Mercutio and Tybalt could be set off, someone who could present saner counsels. Within this framework, Benvolio is presented as sensible and restrained, but loyal and resourceful.

Among the older people in the play, Capulet and the Nurse stand out. Capulet is brilliantly portrayed. He likes to see himself as a benevolent man, an indulgent father and a genial host. He warns Paris that he will follow his daughter's own inclinations about the choice of a husband, and as a host he is generous enough to welcome the son of his old enemy to his accustomed feast. But Shakespeare shows another side to his character when he is crossed by Tybalt in Act 1, Scene v. His judgment is sound, but his language violent and intemperate. So it is that Capulet's later behaviour to Juliet is seen to be 'in character'. His language when faced with opposition from her in Act V, Scene iii, shows him as self-willed, insensitive, and brutal. Such a reaction at this point is vital to the development of the plot – as is the much slighter portrait of Lady Capulet as cold and unsympathetic. The Nurse, who attracts great comic actresses with one of the few plums Shakespeare provides for them, is equally alive. She is earthy and talkative, with a primitive sense of humour. It is consistent in such a character that she should have as little control over her emotions as she has over her tongue. She is warm and affectionate, and it may come as something of a shock when she advises Juliet to abandon Romeo. However this, too, is essential to the plot, and given her straightforward, unromantic ideas, is quite believable. Friar Lawrence, so important in the action of the play, is conventionally drawn. He moralizes, saying all that a religious man should say. He is not without touches of humour, though, and is shown to have a lively affection for his young friend Romeo. Towards the end of the play, Shakespeare perhaps loses interest in him as a character, and his actions are governed by the necessities of the plot.

Plot

Chorus   It is generally no part of the intentions of a Tragedy to be original in its plot: such a work deals most frequently with a story that is well-known to the audience. So it is with *Romeo and Juliet*, and indeed Shakespeare straight away introduces a Chorus to tell us what the play is going to be about.

Act I   The action starts with a street brawl between servants of the two rival families, the Capulets and the Montagues. They are at first rather wary of one another, and fighting only begins when the Capulet pair see Benvolio coming, from whom they expect support. In fact, Benvolio responsibly tries to break up the fight, but Tybalt, far from heeding his call for help in subduing the riotous servants, joins in himself by attacking Benvolio. Some citizens of Verona, evidently weary of the quarrels between the two families, set upon them both impartially. When Capulet and Montague themselves arrive, they are only prevented from drawing swords on one another by their wives. The fighting is at its height when the Prince arrives. Having with some difficulty restored order, he threatens death to any member of either family found in the street disturbances in future. He leaves, taking Capulet with him, Montague remaining behind under instructions to attend the Prince later.

Montague and his wife, relieved that their son Romeo was not involved in the fray, inquire if Benvolio has seen him. It is agreed that he is in a strange and gloomy mood, and Benvolio promises to try to find out the reason. This he does easily enough when his friend joins him: Romeo is in love with a girl who will have nothing to do with him. He rejects Benvolio's advice to look elsewhere.

Capulet returns from his interview with the Prince, and is talking to Paris, who wishes to

marry his daughter, Juliet. Capulet objects th
she is too young for marriage, but nevertheless
he encourages the young nobleman to woo her,
adding that choice of a husband lies entirely with
the girl herself. (We shall see how far from the
truth this really is later in the play). He then
invites Paris to a feast he is holding at his house
that night, where there will be many pretty girls
with whom Paris may compare Juliet. He sends
a servant off with a list of guests upon whom he
must call to deliver the invitations to the feast,
and leaves. The servant, who is unable to read,
seeks the assistance of Romeo in understanding
the list of names he has been given. It includes
the name of Rosaline, the girl whom Romeo
thinks he loves and Benvolio suggests that they
go to the feast, so that Romeo can see that there
are more attractive girls than Rosaline about.
Romeo scorns such an idea, but agrees to go
along. At this feast, a Masked Ball, 'gate-crashers'
were acceptable, as long as they offered some
entertainment to the other guests.

The third scene is given over entirely to the
women. Lady Capulet is trying to tell Juliet that
Paris wishes to marry her, but is constantly
interrupted by the talkative Nurse.

Next, Romeo and Benvolio appear with their
friend Mercutio, discussing the precise way they
will make their entrance at the Masked Ball —
shall they excuse their presence with a speech, or
get straight on with their act, which it seems, is
to be a dance? Romeo declares that he is not in
the mood for dancing, and advises against their
going to the ball, because of a dream he has had.
From the banter that follows this emerges one of
the most famous speeches in the play — Mercutio's
entertaining account about Queen Mab. Romeo
expresses forebodings that there will be some
tragic consequences following the night's revels.

The first Act ends with the scene of the feast

at Capulet's house. The Montague party is welcomed by Capulet, and take part in a dance, but Tybalt recognizes Romeo and, very angry at his presence, sends for his rapier with the intention of fighting. He is restrained by Capulet, who gets equally angry at Tybalt's arguing with him. Tybalt leaves, declaring that he will take some form of revenge on the hated Montague. During the dance, in which Romeo takes no part, he sees Juliet, and falls in love with her, and she with him. They kiss. When the visitors leave, she enquires from the Nurse who the young man that so attracted her is, and discovering that he is a Montague, realizes the impossible position that this, her first love, has put her in.

Act II At the start of the second Act, the Chorus reappears, telling us that Romeo is now in love with someone who returns his love, and that despite the fact that they cannot meet openly, they do contrive to do so in secret.

The first two scenes of this Act are in fact a continuous whole. (You will remember that the division of the play into 'Acts' and 'Scenes' is the work of editors, not of Shakespeare himself.) It is night. Romeo has separated himself from his friends on the way home from the ball, and they are looking for him. Mercutio pretends to try to make Romeo appear by means of a magical incantation, heavily spiced with sexual references. When he and Benvolio go off to bed, Romeo, who has been listening, comes out of hiding. He sees Juliet come out of a room on to her balcony, and hears her speaking about her love for him, despite the quarrel between their families, though wishing he could change his name, so that she might openly declare her love. He interrupts. She is at first frightened at being overheard, then quickly recognizes his voice, and expresses her fears for his safety, should her kinsmen discover him there. The scene then

17

develops into a long exchange between the lovers commonly known as the 'first balcony scene'. The action of the play is advanced to the extent that Juliet promises that if Romeo wishes to marry her, she will come to him, and Romeo proposes to seek the aid of Friar Lawrence to achieve that end.

As dawn breaks, we see Friar Lawrence going about his business of collecting herbs for the making of medicines. Romeo arrives in great haste to ask the Friar to marry Juliet and himself. The Friar, though chiding the young man for his easily changed affections, agrees to do so in the hope that it may bring their two families together, and end the feud in Verona.

Benvolio, Mercutio and Romeo (now in high spirits) are all joking together. Their jesting, which becomes highly improper, is interrupted by the Nurse who is looking for Romeo (she does not know him) with a message from Juliet. She is mocked outrageously by Mercutio, but Romeo eventually gets her to understand that Juliet is to go to Confession at Friar Lawrence's cell that afternoon, where they will be married. His servant will later give the Nurse a rope-ladder which he will use to climb to his wife's room that night.

Juliet is impatiently awaiting the Nurse's return. When she does arrive, she spends some time teasing Juliet, before giving her Romeo's message. Juliet does as she is asked, and Friar Lawrence, after some warning to Romeo of the dangers of violent passion, marries them.

. At this point, the play has had very much the nature of a romantic comedy (apart from several characters' forebodings), with much fun and laughter.

Act III   The next scene, it is important to realize, starts at much the same time as Romeo and Juliet are being married. It is a very hot day – the kind of day on which, as Benvolio remarks, tempers may be lost. He and Mercutio, with some others of the house of Montague, are talking of this very subject, when Tybalt comes in looking for trouble. Mercutio is very ready to match him, and despite restraining words from Benvolio, they are about to fight when Romeo comes along, on his way from the secret marriage ceremony. Tybalt breaks off his quarrel with Mercutio to insult Romeo and to challenge him to a duel. Romeo, now of course a kinsman of the hot-tempered Capulet, turns aside the challenge with an enigmatic remark about the reason he now has to love Tybalt. Mercutio takes this as cowardice, starts a fight with Tybalt, and is fatally wounded when Romeo tries to part them. Tybalt goes out. Mercutio dies. Tybalt returns, and Romeo, furious at the death of his friend, attacks and kills him. Benvolio persuades the bewildered Romeo to run off, as a crowd of citizens, quickly followed by Montague and Capulet and their wives and then by the Prince, come in to see what is going on. Benvolio, called upon to explain what has happened, does his best to defend Romeo's conduct, whilst Lady Capulet demands revenge. The Prince, angry that someone of his own blood has now become a victim of the feud, passes sentence of immediate banishment from Verona on Romeo.

Meanwhile, Juliet is eagerly awaiting the coming of night, looking forward passionately to her first encounter with Romeo as her husband. The Nurse arrives with the terrible news of Romeo's banishment, given in a very confused way because of her distress. Juliet, at first torn between her love for Romeo and her horror that he has killed her cousin Tybalt, gradually realizes how terrible for her is her husband's banishment. The Nurse tells her that she knows where Romeo is, and that he will come to her that night; as planned, to take his farewell.

Friar Lawrence brings to Romeo, who is hiding in his cell, the news of his banishment. Romeo, maddened by grief at being parted from his wife of a few hours, pours out an hysterical torrent of words, and tries to stab himself. He is sternly rebuked by the Friar for unmanliness, then confronted by a plan that he should take refuge in nearby Mantua, while matters are sorted out so that he may return and resume his marriage. The Nurse, who is present during most of this, is deeply impressed by what seems to her the Friar's wisdom, and urges Romeo to make haste to Juliet, as it is getting very late.

There follows a short but very fateful scene, late at night, in which Capulet proposes that Juliet shall marry Paris almost at once, and tells his wife to see that the girl is informed of his decision.

It is now dawn on the following day (you will have noticed how very fast the action of this play moves). Romeo and Juliet have spent a brief night together, and she is at first reluctant to let him go. Romeo eventually climbs down the ladder, and no sooner have they said their unhappy goodbyes than Lady Capulet arrives. Supposing Juliet's tears to be for the death of Tybalt, she breaks what she imagines to be the happy news of the intended marriage to Paris. Juliet, knowing of the impossibility of this, passionately refuses. Capulet, upon entering and hearing of her refusal, rejects the pleas she makes on her knees for a delay, and declares in the most brutal terms that he will, if need be, drag her in a cart to her wedding the following Thursday. Left alone with her Nurse, Juliet seeks her help, only to be advised to forget about Romeo, and go ahead with marriage to the 'lovely gentleman', Paris. Pretending to agree, but bitterly condemning the old woman as soon as she is gone, Juliet decides to seek help from the Friar and, if necessary, to die.

Act IV   At the Friar's cell, after a brief and embarrassing encounter with Paris, who behaves to her in a gracious way, as her husband-to-be, Juliet tells the Friar she will kill herself unless he can find some way out of a bigamous marriage. Restraining her, he produces a plan: he will give her a drug (we now see the point of our first sight of the Friar collecting herbs) which will have the effect of making her appear dead for a period of nearly two days. She will be laid in the vault of the Capulet family, and the Friar himself will send a message to Mantua arranging for Romeo to get to her in the tomb just as consciousness is returning, and to take her away with him. Juliet agrees.

Back at the Capulet home, preparations are going ahead for a wedding feast. Capulet is told that Juliet has gone to confession, and when she returns and asks his pardon for her disobedience, he becomes extremely affable again, expresses his admiration for the good influence of the Friar, and decides to have the wedding brought forward by a day. He goes off to fetch the young bridegroom himself.

Juliet persuades the Nurse and her mother to leave her to herself in her bedroom. As she prepares to drink the drug, she fears that it might not work at all and then that it may be a poison. Terrified by a vision of Tybalt however, she drinks, and the drug takes immediate effect. The Nurse, coming to rouse Juliet for her wedding day, finds her apparently dead. Her screams bring others running in, including the parents, who join the Nurse in expressions of grief. The Friar arrives with Paris, seeks to calm the outbursts, and advises that, 'as the custom is', she shall be carried 'in her best array' to church and then to burial in the tomb.

Act V Romeo is in Mantua. He has had a dream which has left him happy. His servant arrives from Verona with news of Juliet's death and burial. Romeo, grief-stricken, determines, in spite of fate, to return to Verona and die there with his wife. He buys a poison from an apothecary, and sets off for Juliet's tomb.

Back in Verona, the messenger entrusted by Friar Lawrence with a letter of instructions for Romeo returns having been unable to deliver it. The Friar, realizing the dangers of Juliet's awaking alone in the vault, plans at once to go there and release Juliet and to keep her at his cell until he can get in touch with Romeo.

The final scene of the play takes place near and inside the tomb of the Capulets. First to arrive is Paris. He is spreading flowers before the tomb, when his page whistles a warning that someone is coming. It is Romeo with his servant. Dismissing the latter, he sets about breaking open the gates of the vault, but is interrupted by Paris, who had hidden himself. They fight. Paris is killed. Romeo grieves over the body of Juliet, kisses her for the last time, and drinks the poison he has brought with him. No sooner is he dead than Friar Lawrence arrives and discovers his body just as Juliet begins to awake. He tells her what has happened, tries to take her away. She refuses. The Friar, alarmed by the noise of the nightwatchmen, who have been brought to the scene, goes off, and Juliet discovering Romeo dead by her side, uses his dagger to kill herself. Almost at once, the vault begins to fill with people: the watchmen, who have found Friar Lawrence, and Romeo's servant, the Prince, and the Capulets and Montagues. All the story of past events emerges, and Capulet and Montague clasp hands over the bodies of their children – 'poor sacrifices of our enmity'.

Dramatic Structure

It is important to realize that the division into Acts and Scenes of a play by Shakespeare is not necessarily of much help in perceiving its dramatic structure, for such divisions are generally the work of later editors. The action of his plays is much more of, a continuous flow, moving quite across the division into Scenes which you find in this text. A good production of the play ignores such arbitrary divisions when they do not accord with the actual dramatic structure of the piece.

Structurally, the play may usefully be regarded as falling into two parts. The first gives us the background of the. family quarrel in Verona, but then is principally concerned with the courtship of Romeo and Juliet, and ends with their wedding. Despite some brief forebodings of evil to come, the immediate effect of this part as we watch it is that of comedy – it is dominated by merry and entertaining scenes with high-spirited young men, and by the development of love between Romeo and Juliet, with its apparently happy issue in their marriage. Immediately afterwards, in Act III, the mood changes. It is hot and we find 'the mad blood stirring'. Mercutio dies, Tybalt is killed, Romeo is banished, and it becomes clear to us what was meant in the Prologue by the phrase 'a pair of star-cross'd lovers'. Events move with speed to a tragic conclusion.

Within this broad framework, other structural patterns may be discerned. One is an alternation between scenes of a public nature, and those which are of a more private and intimate kind. This, of course, mirrors the interaction in the play between personal relationships, and family and group attitudes. This interaction lies at the very heart of the play, and provides the cause of the tragedy. Thus, the play begins with a very public scene, involving the heads of both quarrelling families, their kinsmen and servants, citizens of Verona, and their ruler himself. This occasion dissolves into a private encounter between Benvolio and Lord and Lady Montague, thence into another between Capulet and Paris, and so to a third between three of the four women of the play. A noisy open air scene with the revellers on their way to the feast is then followed by the feast itself which, though in a private house, has something of the character of a crowded public occasion. The company disperses, and then comes a long intimate meeting in darkness and privacy, between the young lovers, and a brief look at their secret marriage. The second part of the play opens with the second big public scene, involving everyone, as before, including the citizens of Verona and their angry Prince. As before, this is followed by a series of more intimate scenes, but ones in which the fun and supreme happiness of those in the first part of play are replaced by anger, misunderstanding, misery and despair. The deaths of Romeo and Juliet finally call together once again families, citizens and the Prince for the third and last public occasion. The play ends with the public reconciliation, over the bodies of the young, of the quarrels of the old which brought about their deaths.

Other ways of looking at the dramatic structure of the play might concern themselves with the clash between young and old hinted at above, or with the handling of time in the play, or with the carefully placed juxtaposition of dramatic incidents. Or one might look at the different varieties of language in the play, from the essentially lyrical in which little dramatic action is intended, to the language which carries the drama forward.

The truth of the matter is, that for those who admire classical formality, Shakespeare's plays are likely to seem somewhat 'loose' in structure. He does not start out with a structure in mind, but lets one emerge, as the play develops. When we look at the completed work, as with *Romeo and Juliet*, we can find a number of ways of regarding the structure, none of them exclusive.

LIST OF CHARACTERS

CHORUS

ESCALUS *Prince of Verona*

PARIS *a young nobleman, kinsman to the Prince*

MONTAGUE } *heads of two houses at variance*
CAPULET } *with each other*

AN OLD MAN *of the Capulet family*

ROMEO *son to Montague*

MERCUTIO *kinsman to the Prince, and friend to Romeo*

BENVOLIO *nephew to Montague, and friend to Romeo*

TYBALT *nephew to Lady Capulet*

FRIAR LAWRENCE }
FRIAR JOHN } *Franciscans*

BALTHASAR *servant to Romeo*

SAMPSON }
GREGORY } *servants to Capulet*

PETER *servant to Juliet's nurse*

ABRAHAM *servant to Montague*

AN APOTHECARY

THREE MUSICIANS

AN OFFICER

LADY MONTAGUE *wife to Montague*

LADY CAPULET *wife to Capulet*

JULIET *daughter to Capulet*

NURSE *to Juliet*

CITIZENS of VERONA; GENTLEMEN *and* GENTLEWOMEN *of both houses*; MASKERS, TORCHBEARERS, PAGES, GUARDS, WATCHMEN, SERVANTS, *and* ATTENDANTS

THE SCENE: *Verona and Mantua*

NOTES

ACT ONE

THE PROLOGUE

This is an introduction to the play spoken by one of the actors and in this case he tells us, in general terms, what the plot of the play is going to be.

2. *Verona:* a town in Italy.

3. 'Their old quarrel erupts into new violence.'

4. *civil blood:* blood shed in fighting between people of the same town.

6. *star-cross'd:* lovers who are ill-fated because of the influence of the stars. In those days it was widely believed that people's lives were affected by the position of the stars when they were born. Thus Shakespeare tells us, at the very beginning, that the love of Romeo and Juliet will come to a tragic end, not because of their own faults but because it is destined to do so.

9. *death-mark'd:* marked out for death, This phrase emphasizes the warning that they are doomed.

11. *but:* except for.

12. *two hours' traffic:* Elizabethan plays usually lasted about this time: the words were probably said briskly and there was no stage-shifting to waste time.

14. Whatever may be inadequate—whether in the play or in the performance is not clear—the actors will try to make up for by their hard work.

THE PROLOGUE

Enter CHORUS

Two households, both alike in dignity,
In fair Verona, where we lay our scene,
From ancient grudge break to new mutiny,
Where civil blood makes civil hands unclean.
From forth the fatal loins of these two foes   5
A pair of star-cross'd lovers take their life;
Whose misadventur'd piteous overthrows
Doth with their death bury their parents' strife.
The fearful passage of their death-mark'd love,
And the continuance of their parents' rage,   10
Which, but their children's end, nought could remove,
Is now the two hours' traffic of our stage;
The which if you with patient ears attend,
What here shall miss, our toil shall strive to mend.

Exit

At once, Shakespeare indulges in the kind of quibbling with words that is common in the play. Much of it here, spoken by the serving men, is crude and vulgar.

1. *carry coals:* do menial work.

2. *colliers:* coal-miners. Gregory takes Sampson's phrase in its literal rather than figurative sense.

3. *choler:* anger. The word puns backward to *collier* and forward to *collar* in line 4.
draw: draw their swords. Gregory puns on this with the phrase: *draw your neck out of collar* in line 4.
4. *collar:* hangman's noose.

5-10. There follows a series of puns on the word *move*, meaning in lines 5 and 7 'made angry', in lines 6 and 10 'given cause to', and in lines 8 and 9 'to change position'.

10-11. *take the wall:* walk nearest the wall: an aggressive action, forcing anyone passing to walk nearest the road and thus run the risk of being splashed with mud.

12-13. *goes to the wall:* is pushed into an inferior position.

ACT ONE

Verona. A public place

Enter SAMPSON *and* GREGORY, *of the house of Capulet, with swords and bucklers on*

Sampson
  Gregory, on my word, we'll not carry coals.
Gregory
  No, for then we should be colliers.
Sampson
  I mean, an we be in choler, we'll draw.
Gregory
  Ay, while you live, draw your neck out of collar.
Sampson
  I strike quickly, being moved. 5
Gregory
  But thou art not quickly moved to strike.
Sampson
  A dog of the house of Montague moves me.
Gregory
  To move is to stir, and to be valiant is to stand;
  therefore, if thou art moved, thou run'st away.
Sampson
  A dog of that house shall move me to stand. I will take 10
  the wall of any man or maid of Montague's.
Gregory
  That shows thee a weak slave; for the weakest goes
  to the wall.
Sampson
  'Tis true; and therefore women, being the weaker
  vessels, are ever thrust to the wall; therefore I will 15
  push Montague's men from the wall and thrust his
  maids to the wall.

18. Gregory pretends to rebuke Sampson saying that the quarrel is between men and that women are not involved.

23. *maidenheads :* state of virginity.

24-5. Gregory and Sampson quibble on the word *sense*, meaning in line 24 'meaning' and in line 25 'feeling'.

26-7. Sampson says that he will make their women feel him as long as he can maintain an erection, and it's well known how effective he is in that way!

29. *poor-John:* dried hake, a very unpalatable dish.

35. *Let us take the law of our sides:* Let us make sure we are on the right side of the law.' Gregory and Sampson are not really so bold as they like to pretend.

38. *bite my thumb:* an insulting gesture at that time—the clicking of the thumbnail against the teeth.

Gregory
  The quarrel is between our masters and us their men.
Sampson
  'Tis all one; I will show myself a tyrant. When I have
  fought with the men, I will be civil with the maids—   *20*
  I will cut off their heads.
Gregory
  The heads of the maids?
Sampson
  Ay, the heads of the maids, or their maidenheads;
  take it in what sense thou wilt.
Gregory
  They must take it in sense that feel it.   *25*
Sampson
  Me they shall feel while I am able to stand; and 'tis
  known I am a pretty piece of flesh.
Gregory
  'Tis well thou art not fish; if thou hadst, thou hadst
  been poor-John. Draw thy tool; here comes two of
  the house of Montagues.   *30*
  Enter two other Servingmen, ABRAHAM *and* BALTHASAR
Sampson
  My naked weapon is out; quarrel, I will back thee.
Gregory
  How? turn thy back and run?
Sampson
  Fear me not.
Gregory
  No, marry; I fear thee!
Sampson
  Let us take the law of our sides; let them begin.   *35*
Gregory
  I will frown as I pass by, and let them take it as they
  list.
Sampson
  Nay, as they dare. I will bite my thumb at them,
  which is disgrace to them if they bear it.

53. Gregory urges Sampson to claim that Capulet is a better man than Montague; he feels it is safe to be bolder because he sees Tybalt coming, who he thinks will support them.

57. *swashing:* swishing, sweeping.

Abraham
　Do you bite your thumb at us, sir?　　　　　*40*

Sampson
　I do bite my thumb, sir.

Abraham
　Do you bite your thumb at us, sir?

Sampson [*Aside to* GREGORY]
　Is the law of our side, if I say ay?

Gregory [*Aside to* SAMPSON]
　No.

Sampson
　No, sir, I do not bite my thumb at you, sir; but I bite　*45*
　my thumb, sir.

Gregory
　Do you quarrel, sir?

Abraham
　Quarrel, sir! No, sir.

Sampson
　But if you do, sir, I am for you. I serve as good a
　man as you.　　　　　*50*

Abraham
　No better?

Sampson
　Well, sir.

Enter BENVOLIO

Gregory [*Aside to* SAMPSON]
　Say 'better'; here comes one of my master's kinsmen.

Sampson
　Yes, better, sir.

Abraham
　You lie.　　　　　*55*

Sampson
　Draw, if you be men. Gregory, remember thy
　swashing blow.

They fight

33

60-6. Benvolio tries to stop the servants fighting; but when Tybalt enters, he forces Benvolio into a fight himself; so begins the 'new mutiny' of the Prologue.

60. *heartless hinds:* a complicated pun (*hind* = deer and servant). Presumably the hind is to be regarded as a symbol of timidity.

67. *bills, and partisans:* long-handled weapons.

Benvolio
  Part, fools!   *Beats down their swords*
  Put up your swords; you know not what you do.

                    Enter TYBALT

Tybalt
  What, art thou drawn among these heartless hinds?   *60*
  Turn thee, Benvolio; look upon thy death.
Benvolio
  I do but keep the peace; put up thy sword,
  Or manage it to part these men with me.
Tybalt
  What, drawn, and talk of peace! I hate the word,
  As I hate hell, all Montagues, and thee.   *65*
  Have at thee, coward!

                    They fight.

  Enter an OFFICER, *and three or four* CITIZENS *with
              clubs or partisans*

Officer
  Clubs, bills, and partisans! Strike; beat them down.
Citizens
  Down with the Capulets! Down with the Montagues!
        Enter OLD CAPULET *in his gown, and his* WIFE
Capulet
  What noise is this? Give me my long sword, ho!
Lady Capulet
  A crutch, a crutch! Why call you for a sword?   *70*
Capulet
  My sword, I say! Old Montague is come,
  And flourishes his blade in spite of me.

            Enter OLD MONTAGUE *and his* WIFE

Montague
  Thou villain Capulet!—Hold me not, let me go.
Lady Montague
  Thou shalt not stir one foot to seek a foe.

            Enter PRINCE ESCALUS *with his* TRAIN

76. *neighbour-stained:* stained with the blood of neighbours.

81. *mistempered:* used in a wrong cause.

86-9. The Prince says that the old citizens of Verona have had to intervene to break up the quarrels between the parties of Montague and Capulet.
87. *grave beseeming ornaments:* the sober equipment of peaceful men.
89. *Canker'd . . . canker'd:* (1) age-stiffened; (2) malignant.

98. *abroach:* open (a term usually applied to a barrel).

104-6. Benvolio speaks with contempt of Tybalt's showy behaviour.

Prince

Rebellious subjects, enemies to peace,   *75*
Profaners of this neighbour-stained steel—
Will they not hear? What, ho! you men, you beasts,
That quench the fire of your pernicious rage
With purple fountains issuing from your veins!
On pain of torture, from those bloody hands   *80*
Throw your mistempered weapons to the ground,
And hear the sentence of your moved prince.
Three civil brawls, bred of an airy word,
By thee, old Capulet, and Montague,
Have thrice disturb'd the quiet of our streets   *85*
And made Verona's ancient citizens
Cast by their grave beseeming ornaments
To wield old partisans, in hands as old,
Canker'd with peace, to part your canker'd hate.
If ever you disturb our streets again,   *90*
Your lives shall pay the forfeit of the peace.
For this time all the rest depart away.
You, Capulet, shall go along with me;
And, Montague, come you this afternoon,
To know our farther pleasure in this case,   *95*
To old Free-town, our common judgment-place.
Once more, on pain of death, all men depart.

Exeunt all but MONTAGUE, *his* WIFE, *and* BENVOLIO

Montague

Who set this ancient quarrel new abroach?
Speak, nephew; were you by when it began?

Benvolio

Here were the servants of your adversary   *100*
And yours, close fighting ere I did approach.
I drew to part them; in the instant came
The fiery Tybalt, with his sword prepar'd;
Which, as he breath'd defiance to my ears,
He swung about his head and cut the winds,   *105*
Who, nothing hurt withal, hiss'd him in scorn.

108. *on part and part:* on either side.

112. Note that the tone of the language here changes from that of violence to a song-like, decorative style.

119. *covert:* shade, cover.
120. *measuring his affections by my own:* 'judging his mood by what I know of my own.'
121. 'which at that time inclined me to be alone.'

123. 'followed my own inclination not to break in upon his desire to be alone.'

126. *augmenting:* adding to.

129-31. An elaborate way of describing the sunrise, in keeping with the change in the style of the language mentioned in the note to line 112.
130. *Aurora:* in Roman mythology, the goddess of the dawn.
131. *heavy:* heavy-hearted.

135. 'this mood suggests a gloomy outcome.'

While we were interchanging thrusts and blows,
Came more and more, and fought on part and part,
Till the Prince came, who parted either part.

Lady Montague

O, where is Romeo? Saw you him to-day?   *110*
Right glad I am he was not at this fray.

Benvolio

Madam, an hour before the worshipp'd sun
Peer'd forth the golden window of the east,
A troubled mind drew me to walk abroad;
Where, underneath the grove of sycamore   *115*
That westward rooteth from this city side,
So early walking did I see your son.
Towards him I made; but he was ware of me
And stole into the covert of the wood.
I, measuring his affections by my own,   *120*
Which then most sought where most might not be
      found,
Being one too many by my weary self,
Pursu'd my humour, not pursuing his,
And gladly shunn'd who gladly fled from me.

Montague

Many a morning hath he there been seen,   *125*
With tears augmenting the fresh morning's dew,
Adding to clouds more clouds with his deep sighs;
But all so soon as the all-cheering sun
Should in the farthest east begin to draw
The shady curtains from Aurora's bed,   *130*
Away from light steals home my heavy son,
And private in his chamber pens himself,
Shuts up his windows, locks fair daylight out,
And makes himself an artificial night.
Black and portentous must this humour prove,   *135*
Unless good counsel may the cause remove.

Benvolio

My noble uncle, do you know the cause?

139. *importun'd:* urged him to explain his behaviour.

141 *his own affections' counsellor:* suggests that Romeo will be guided only by his own inclinations, which are to keep his affairs very strictly to himself.

144. *sounding and discovery:* submitting to questions, and answering them.

152-3. 'I hope that you will be so fortunate by staying behind as to get a true confession out of him.'

Montague
I neither know it nor can learn of him.
Benvolio
Have you importun'd him by any means?
Montague
Both by myself and many other friends.   *140*
But he, his own affections' counsellor,
Is to himself—I will not say how true;
But to himself so secret and so close,
So far from sounding and discovery,
As is the bud bit with an envious worm,   *145*
Ere he can spread his sweet leaves to the air,
Or dedicate his beauty to the sun.
Could we but learn from whence his sorrows grow,
We would as willingly give cure as know.

Enter ROMEO

Benvolio
See where he comes. So please you step aside;   *150*
I'll know his grievance or be much denied.
Montague
I would thou wert so happy by thy stay
To hear true shrift. Come, madam, let's away.

Exeunt MONTAGUE *and his* WIFE

Benvolio
Good morrow, cousin.
Romeo   Is the day so young?
Benvolio
But new struck nine.
Romeo   Ay me! sad hours seem long.   *155*
Was that my father that went hence so fast?
Benvolio
It was. What sadness lengthens Romeo's hours?
Romeo
Not having that which having makes them short.

160. 'out of favour with the girl I'm in love with.'

163-4. 'Alas that love, which seems so attractive in prospect, turns out to be so harsh in practice.'

165. *Alas that love, whose view is muffled . . .:* Romeo is here referring to Cupid, the archer of love in Roman mythology who was always pictured as blind, but who is nevertheless able to get his own way with us (*see pathways to his will*).

167. *O me! What fray was here?* Romeo presumably notices the weapons lying on the ground and goes on to lament the social disorder in a series of contradictory phrases (oxymorons). The over-elaborateness of the language suits Romeo's present superficial form of romantic love.

178. 'at your being so heavy-hearted.'

179. Romeo replies that this is the common effect that being in love has on one. (We may contrast this superficial infatuation with the profound passion that Romeo will feel for Juliet, after meeting her.)

180-2. 'I am weighed down by my own troubles, which will only be increased if you show distress.'

Benvolio
    In love?
Romeo
    Out—   *160*
Benvolio
    Of love?
Romeo
    Out of her favour where I am in love.
Benvolio
    Alas that love, so gentle in his view,
    Should be so tyrannous and rough in proof!
Romeo
    Alas that love, whose view is muffled still,   *165*
    Should without eyes see pathways to his will!
    Where shall we dine? O me! What fray was here?
    Yet tell me not, for I have heard it all.
    Here's much to do with hate, but more with love.
    Why then, O brawling love! O loving hate!   *170*
    O anything, of nothing first create!
    O heavy lightness! serious vanity!
    Mis-shapen chaos of well-seeming forms!
    Feather of lead, bright smoke, cold fire, sick health!
    Still-waking sleep, that is not what it is!   *175*
    This love feel I, that feel no love in this.
    Dost thou not laugh?
Benvolio   No, coz, I rather weep.
Romeo
    Good heart, at what?
Benvolio   At thy good heart's oppression.
Romeo
    Why, such is love's transgression.
    Griefs of mine own lie heavy in my breast,   *180*
    Which thou wilt propagate, to have it prest
    With more of thine. This love that thou hast shown
    Doth add more grief to too much of mine own.
    Love is a smoke rais'd with the fume of sighs;
    Being purg'd, a fire sparkling in lovers' eyes;   *185*

187. *discreet:* discriminating—another forced paradox, since madness usually implies an inability to make discriminating judgements. In this speech Romeo continues to play with words and act the conventional part of the distracted lover.

188. *gall:* bitterness, poison.

193. *in sadness:* in all seriousness.

195. *sadly:* seriously.

196. *in sadness:* a pun, introducing the more modern meaning of 'unhappiness'.

197. Romeo goes on to say that, with this meaning, the word is an unfortunate one to use to a man who is sick, i.e. with love.

201. *A right fair mark:* an easily seen target.

203. *Dian's wit:* she has the cleverness of Diana (the Roman goddess of chastity) in avoiding the temptations of love and remaining a virgin.

206. *stay:* give in to.

207. *bide:* put up with.

208. She will not give up her virginity even for gold, capable of seducing saints.

210. Because she will have no children to perpetuate her beauty (*store* = fertility, increase). This idea is restated in lines 213 and 214, and is a common one in Elizabethan poetry. Elizabethan ladies often wore black masks when they walked in public places.

Being vex'd, a sea nourish'd with loving tears.
What is it else? A madness most discreet,
A choking gall, and a preserving sweet.
Farewell, my coz.

Benvolio   Soft! I will go along;
  An if you leave me so, you do me wrong.   *190*

Romeo
  Tut, I have lost myself; I am not here:
  This is not Romeo, he's some other where.

Benvolio
  Tell me in sadness who is that you love.

Romeo
  What, shall I groan and tell thee?

Benvolio   Groan! Why, no;
  But sadly tell me who.   *195*

Romeo
  Bid a sick man in sadness make his will.
  Ah, word ill urg'd to one that is so ill!
  In sadness, cousin, I do love a woman.

Benvolio
  I aim'd so near when I suppos'd you lov'd.

Romeo
  A right good markman! And she's fair I love.   *200*

Benvolio
  A right fair mark, fair coz, is soonest hit.

Romeo
  Well, in that hit you miss: she'll not be hit
  With Cupid's arrow. She hath Dian's wit,
  And in strong proof of chastity well arm'd,
  From Love's weak childish bow she lives unharm'd. *205*
  She will not stay the siege of loving terms,
  Nor bide th' encounter of assailing eyes,
  Nor ope her lap to saint-seducing gold.
  O, she is rich in beauty; only poor
  That, when she dies, with beauty dies her store.   *210*

Benvolio
  Then she hath sworn that she will still live chaste?

229-30. Romeo says that looking at other women only heightens and emphasizes her beauty in his eyes.

232. *I'll pay that doctrine:* I'll teach you that lesson.

SCENE II

It is clear at the beginning of this scene, that Capulet and Paris have been discussing the Duke's warning that the family quarrel between the Montagues and the Capulets must stop.

Romeo

   She hath, and in that sparing makes huge waste;
   For beauty, starv'd with her severity,
   Cuts beauty off from all posterity.
   She is too fair, too wise, wisely too fair,   *215*
   To merit bliss by making me despair.
   She hath forsworn to love, and in that vow
   Do I live dead that live to tell it now.

Benvolio

   Be rul'd by me: forget to think of her.

Romeo

   O teach me how I should forget to think!   *220*

Benvolio

   By giving liberty unto thine eyes.
   Examine other beauties.

Romeo   'Tis the way
   To call hers, exquisite, in question more.
   These happy masks that kiss fair ladies' brows,
   Being black, puts us in mind they hide the fair.   *225*
   He that is strucken blind cannot forget
   The precious treasure of his eyesight lost.
   Show me a mistress that is passing fair,
   What doth her beauty serve but as a note
   Where I may read who pass'd that passing fair?   *230*
   Farewell; thou canst not teach me to forget.

Benvolio

   I'll pay that doctrine or else die in debt.

                    Exeunt

SCENE II—*A street*

     Enter CAPULET, COUNTY PARIS, *and the* CLOWN,
                 his servant

Capulet

   But Montague is bound as well as I,
   In penalty alike; and 'tis not hard, I think,
   For men so old as we to keep the peace.

6. *my suit:* Paris is evidently seeking to marry Juliet.

9. 'She is not yet fourteen.' Girls have always tended to marry young in Mediterranean countries. Nevertheless, Capulet would prefer his daughter to be a couple of years older before she has a husband.

14. Capulet's other children are dead and buried and all his hopes are centred upon Juliet.

17. Capulet is saying that he is quite willing to fall in with Juliet's own decision; of course, he takes a very different view later on!

25. *Earth-treading stars:* extremely pretty girls—goddesses on earth, as it were.

29. *fresh female buds:* girls who have not yet blossomed into woman-hood.
30. *Inherit:* enjoy, receive as your own.

32-3. He says that Paris will that evening see Juliet among all the other girls and then he may, or may not, think her the best.

Paris

  Of honourable reckoning are you both,
  And pity 'tis you liv'd at odds so long.   5
  But now, my lord, what say you to my suit?
Capulet

  But saying o'er what I have said before:
  My child is yet a stranger in the world,
  She hath not seen the change of fourteen years;
  Let two more summers wither in their pride   10
  Ere we may think her ripe to be a bride.
Paris

  Younger than she are happy mothers made.
Capulet

  And too soon marr'd are those so early made.
  Earth hath swallowed all my hopes but she;
  She is the hopeful lady of my earth.   15
  But woo her, gentle Paris, get her heart;
  My will to her consent is but a part.
  And, she agreed, within her scope of choice
  Lies my consent and fair according voice.
  This night I hold an old accustom'd feast,   20
  Whereto I have invited many a guest,
  Such as I love; and you among the store,
  One more, most welcome, makes my number more.
  At my poor house look to behold this night
  Earth-treading stars that make dark heaven light.   25
  Such comfort as do lusty young men feel
  When well-apparell'd April on the heel
  Of limping winter treads, even such delight
  Among fresh female buds shall you this night
  Inherit at my house. Hear all, all see,   30
  And like her most whose merit most shall be;
  Which on more view of many, mine, being one,
  May stand in number, though in reck'ning none.
  Come, go with me. [*To* SERVANT, *giving him a paper*] Go,
      sirrah, trudge about
  Through fair Verona; find those persons out   35

39-44. The servant, evidently a comically stupid figure, gets into a muddle: it is the tailor who uses a yard, the shoemaker a last, the fisher a net and the painter a pencil.

44. He goes off to find an educated person who can read the list for him.

45-50. Benvolio is again advising Romeo to find another girl for this will cure him of the pain of his present infatuation.

48. *languish:* disease.

50. *rank:* strong.

51. A plantain leaf was supposed to be a remedy for a sore shin; Romeo scornfully dismisses Benvolio's remedy for love by implying that love-sickness cannot be cured as easily as a cut shin.

54. *but bound more than a madman is:* it was an Elizabethan custom to keep madmen tied up and shut away.

58. 'I can see what my future is going to be by examining my present unhappiness.'

Whose names are written there, and to them say
My house and welcome on their pleasure stay.

Exeunt CAPULET *and* PARIS

Servant

Find them out whose names are written here! It is
written that the shoemaker should meddle with his
yard and the tailor with his last, the fisher with his   *40*
pencil and the painter with his nets; but I am sent to
find those persons whose names are here writ, and
can never find what names the writing person hath
here writ. I must to the learned. In good time!

Enter BENVOLIO *and* ROMEO

Benvolio

Tut, man, one fire burns out another's burning,   *45*
One pain is less'ned by another's anguish;
Turn giddy, and be holp by backward turning;
One desperate grief cures with another's languish.
Take thou some new infection to thy eye,
And the rank poison of the old will die.   *50*

Romeo

Your plantain leaf is excellent for that.

Benvolio

For what, I pray thee?

Romeo   For your broken shin.

Benvolio

Why, Romeo, art thou mad?

Romeo

Not mad, but bound more than a madman is;
Shut up in prison, kept without my food,   *55*
Whipt and tormented, and—God-den, good fellow.

Servant

God gi' go'den. I pray, sir, can you read?

Romeo

Ay, mine own fortune in my misery.

59. *without book:* by listening to a teacher.

62. The simple-minded servant fails to understand Romeo's elaborate way of saying yes.

81. *crush:* try the quality by drinking it.

Servant
Perhaps you have learned it without book. But I
pray, can you read anything you see?   *60*

Romeo
Ay, if I know the letters and the language.

Servant
Ye say honestly; rest you merry!

Romeo
Stay, fellow; I can read.
[*He reads the list*] 'Signior Martino and his wife and
daughters; County Anselme and his beauteous sis-   *65*
ters; the lady widow of Vitruvio; Signior Placentio
and his lovely nieces; Mercutio and his brother Valen-
tine; mine uncle Capulet, his wife, and daughters;
my fair niece Rosaline and Livia; Signior Valentio
and his cousin Tybalt; Lucio and the lively Helena.'   *70*
A fair assembly. [*Gives back the paper*] Whither
should they come?

Servant
Up.

Romeo
Whither?

Servant
To supper. To our house.   *75*

Romeo
Whose house?

Servant
My master's.

Romeo
Indeed, I should have ask'd you that before.

Servant
Now I'll tell you without asking: my master is the
great rich Capulet; and if you be not of the house of   *80*
Montagues, I pray come and crush a cup of wine.
Rest you merry!

Exit

86. *unattainted:* unprejudiced.

89-92. 'When my eyes are so faithless to my belief in the superiority of Rosaline, may they, like heretics who reject the true faith, be burnt.'

91. *And these:* i.e. his eyes.
often drown'd: i.e. with tears of sorrow.

97. *crystal scales:* Romeo's two eyes.

100. *scant:* scarcely.

102. *splendour of mine own:* the splendour of Rosaline.

SCENE III

2. The Nurse swears by her virginity at twelve years old—presumably she lost it soon after!

Benvolio

  At this same ancient feast of Capulet's

  Sups the fair Rosaline whom thou so loves,

  With all the admired beauties of Verona.   *85*

  Go thither, and with unattainted eye

  Compare her face with some that I shall show,

  And I will make thee think thy swan a crow.

Romeo

  When the devout religion of mine eye

  Maintains such falsehood, then turn tears to fires;   *90*

  And these, who, often drown'd, could never die,

  Transparent heretics, be burnt for liars!

  One fairer than my love! The all-seeing sun

  Ne'er saw her match since first the world begun.

Benvolio

  Tut, you saw her fair, none else being by,   *95*

  Herself pois'd with herself in either eye;

  But in that crystal scales let there be weigh'd

  Your lady's love against some other maid

  That I will show you shining at this feast,

  And she shall scant show well that now seems best.   *100*

Romeo

  I'll go along, no such sight to be shown,

  But to rejoice in splendour of mine own.

Exeunt

SCENE III—*Capulet's house*

Enter LADY CAPULET *and* NURSE

Lady Capulet

  Nurse, where's my daughter? Call her forth to me.

Nurse

  Now, by my maidenhead at twelve year old,

  I bade her come. What, lamb! what, ladybird!

  God forbid! Where's this girl? What, Juliet!

14. *teen:* sorrow; even the Nurse is punning, on the word 'fourteen'.

16. *Lammas-tide:* 1st August.

18. Juliet's youth is stressed.

19-21. Susan was the Nurse's own daughter, born at the same time as Juliet and because of whom the Nurse was able to suckle Juliet. Evidently she died in infancy.

27. The Nurse had put wormwood, a bitter herb, upon her nipple to discourage the baby from taking milk. This kind of detail is in keeping with the earthy character of the Nurse.

30. *Nay, I do bear a brain:* 'My, I am clever.' The Nurse's pride in her memory and her prattling on and on give us a very real impression of a talkative old woman.

Enter JULIET

Juliet
  How now, who calls?   5
Nurse
  Your mother.
Juliet
  Madam, I am here. What is your will?
Lady Capulet
  This is the matter. Nurse, give leave awhile,
  We must talk in secret. Nurse, come back again;
  I have remember'd me, thou's hear our counsel.   10
  Thou knowest my daughter's of a pretty age.
Nurse
  Faith, I can tell her age unto an hour.
Lady Capulet
  She's not fourteen.
Nurse   I'll lay fourteen of my teeth—
  And yet, to my teen be it spoken, I have but four—
  She's not fourteen. How long is it now   15
  To Lammas-tide?
Lady Capulet   A fortnight and odd days.
Nurse
  Even or odd, of all days in the year,
  Come Lammas Eve at night shall she be fourteen.
  Susan and she—God rest all Christian souls!—
  Were of an age. Well, Susan is with God;   20
  She was too good for me. But, as I said,
  On Lammas Eve at night shall she be fourteen;
  That shall she, marry; I remember it well.
  'Tis since the earthquake now eleven years;
  And she was wean'd—I never shall forget it—   25
  Of all the days of the year, upon that day;
  For I had then laid wormwood to my dug,
  Sitting in the sun under the dove-house wall;
  My lord and you were then at Mantua.
  Nay, I do bear a brain. But, as I said,   30
  When it did taste the wormwood on the nipple

[handwritten annotation: Nurses daughter]

[handwritten annotation: likes to hear the sound of her own voice]

33. *tetchy:* cross.

34. *Shake, quoth the dove-house.* The Nurse weaned Juliet, as she has said, on the day of the earthquake, sitting by the dovehouse wall (*dove-house:* a nesting place for doves usually on top of a pole). Evidently the earthquake occurred as she was sitting there and the dovehouse began to rock (she personifies the building, making it say 'shake'). Her fear of its collapse was sufficient to send her scuttling for safety, as she says: '*Twas no need, I trow, To bid me trudge.*'

37. *high-lone:* quite alone, without support.

by th' rood: by the Holy Cross on which Christ died.

39. *broke her brow:* cut her forehead.

43. The husband says that when Juliet is grown-up, she will fall on her back under a lover rather than on her face. He appears to have been just as vulgar a character as the Nurse is.

44. *by my holidam:* This was originally an oath sworn on holy relics, but had come to be thought of as a reference to the Virgin Mary.

40–49. One can imagine the Nurse saying these words accompanied by loud guffaws of laughter.

49. *stinted:* stopped crying.

53. *it:* the old form of 'its'.

54. *stone:* testicle. This part of a young cockerel is remarkably large. This is the kind of metaphor one would expect the Nurse to use.

62. *once:* some day.

Of my dug, and felt it bitter, pretty fool,
To see it tetchy, and fall out with the dug!
Shake, quoth the dove-house. 'Twas no need, I trow,
To bid me trudge.   35
And since that time it is eleven years;
For then she could stand high-lone; nay, by th' rood,
She could have run and waddled all about;
For even the day before, she broke her brow;
And then my husband—God be with his soul!   40
'A was a merry man—took up the child.
'Yea,' quoth he 'dost thou fall upon thy face?
Thou wilt fall backward when thou hast more wit,
Wilt thou not, Jule?' And, by my holidam,
The pretty wretch left crying, and said 'Ay'.   45
To see, now, how a jest shall come about!
I warrant, an I should live a thousand years,
I never should forget it: 'Wilt thou not, Jule?' quoth he;
And, pretty fool, it stinted, and said 'Ay'.

Lady Capulet
  Enough of this; I pray thee hold thy peace.   50
Nurse
  Yes, madam. Yet I cannot choose but laugh
To think it should leave crying and say 'Ay'.
And yet, I warrant, it had upon it brow
A bump as big as a young cock'rel's stone—
A perilous knock; and it cried bitterly.   55
'Yea,' quoth my husband 'fall'st upon thy face?
Thou wilt fall backward when thou comest to age;
Wilt thou not, Jule?' It stinted, and said 'Ay'.

Juliet
  And stint thou too, I pray thee, nurse, say I.
Nurse
  Peace, I have done. God mark thee to his grace!   60
Thou wast the prettiest babe that e'er I nurs'd;
An I might live to see thee married once,
I have my wish.

64. The first *Marry* is the common oath, meaning 'by the Virgin Mary'.

69. Unusual modesty on the Nurse's part.

72-4. 'By my reckoning, you were already born when I was your age.'

77. *a man of wax:* a perfect figure of a man.

82-93. Lady Capulet praises Paris, in an extended image, speaking of him as if he were a fine book.

84. *married lineament:* features that set one another off well.

87. *margent:* margin. His eyes are compared to a note in the margin of the book; this elaborate imagery does not seem to have very much meaning, except that possibly Lady Capulet means that one can read Paris' character by looking into his eyes.
88. *unbound:* unmarried.
89. *a cover:* a wife.
90-1. Just as the sea is proud of containing beautiful fish, so Juliet (the cover) should be proud to have the beautiful Paris (the book) as her husband.

Lady Capulet
  Marry, that 'marry' is the very theme
  I came to talk of. Tell me, daughter Juliet,   *65*
  How stands your dispositions to be married?
Juliet
  It is an honour that I dream not of.
Nurse
  An honour! Were not I thine only nurse,
  I would say thou hadst suck'd wisdom from thy teat.
Lady Capulet
  Well, think of marriage now. Younger than you,   *70*
  Here in Verona, ladies of esteem,
  Are made already mothers. By my count,
  I was your mother much upon these years
  That you are now a maid. Thus, then, in brief:
  The valiant Paris seeks you for his love.   *75*
Nurse
  A man, young lady! lady, such a man
  As all the world—why, he's a man of wax.
Lady Capulet
  Verona's summer hath not such a flower.
Nurse
  Nay, he's a flower; in faith, a very flower.
Lady Capulet
  What say you? Can you love the gentleman?   *80*
  This night you shall behold him at our feast;
  Read o'er the volume of young Paris' face,
  And find delight writ there with beauty's pen;
  Examine every married lineament,
  And see how one another lends content;   *85*
  And what obscur'd in this fair volume lies
  Find written in the margent of his eyes.
  This precious book of love, this unbound lover,
  To beautify him, only lacks a cover.
  The fish lives in the sea, and 'tis much pride   *90*
  For fair without the fair within to hide.

92-3. That is, Juliet, as Paris' wife, would share his eminence.

96. The Nurse cannot miss this opportunity for a bawdy jest; she means that women grow larger when they are pregnant.

98. 'I will be prepared to like him, if I find him attractive to look at.'
99-100. Juliet says dutifully that she will only commit herself as far as her mother allows or desires.

103. *in extremity:* in utter confusion

105. *County:* Count, i.e. Paris.

106. Inevitably, the Nurse's thoughts run to the pleasures of lovers in bed.

SCENE IV

The young men are on their way to the Capulet's ball: they propose to push their way in uninvited wearing comic masks, which was an accepted social custom of the time. They also propose to give an entertainment of their own.

1-2. They have prepared, as was the custom, a short speech, to be spoken on their entry, explaining their intrusion.

3. Benvolio says that such speeches are out of date and unfashionable. *prolixity:* long-windedness.

That book in many's eyes doth share the glory
That in gold clasps locks in the golden story;
So shall you share all that he doth possess,
By having him making yourself no less.   95

Nurse

No less! Nay, bigger; women grow by men.

Lady Capulet

Speak briefly, can you like of Paris' love?

Juliet

I'll look to like, if looking liking move; — *if you want me to marry I will.*
But no more deep will I endart mine eye
Than your consent gives strength to make it fly.   100

Enter a SERVANT

Servant

Madam, the guests are come, supper serv'd up, you
call'd, my young lady ask'd for, the nurse curs'd in
the pantry, and everything in extremity. I must hence
to wait; I beseech you, follow straight.

Lady Capulet

We follow thee. [*Exit* SERVANT] Juliet, the County   105
stays.

Nurse

Go, girl, seek happy nights to happy days.

Exeunt

SCENE IV—*A street*

Enter ROMEO, MERCUTIO, BENVOLIO, *with five or
six other* MASKERS; TORCH-BEARERS

Romeo

What, shall this speech be spoke for our excuse?
Or shall we on without apology?

Benvolio

The date is out of such prolixity.

63

4-6. It would appear that such speeches were sometimes spoken by a character dressed up, for instance, as a blind Cupid, and that sometimes the ladies were frightened by such an apparition.

4. *hoodwink'd:* blindfolded.

5. The Tartars were traditionally armed with lip-shaped bows, such as Cupid bore.

of lath: of thin wood; that is, this bow is only a stage prop.

6. *crow-keeper:* a boy employed to scare crows.

7-8. *no without-book prologue . . . entrance:* an introductory speech made haltingly without a script and with much assistance from the prompter, the person who reminds or helps out an actor who has forgotten his words.

9. 'Let them think what they like of us.'

10. We shall dance a dance for them and then leave.

12. *heavy:* heavy-hearted because of his unrequited love for Rosaline.

15. *soles . . . soul:* a characteristic pun

18-21. Mercutio and Romeo pun heavily on the words *soar* (fly), *sore* (painfully), *bound* (tied down) and *bound* (leap).

22. 'I am weighed down by the pain of love.'

23-4. Mercutio characteristically perverts Romeo's previous words and gives them a directly sexual meaning. He says that to perform the sexual act (*to sink in it*) Romeo must be a weight on the woman (*love*) lying underneath him.

27-8. Mercutio suggests that if Romeo feels the pain of love he should give vent to his sexual desire, and so relieve the pain through the sexual act.

29. *a case:* a mask.

30. 'An (ugly) false face to cover my (ugly) real one.'

31. *curious:* inquisitive; *quote:* observe.

32. He points to the extravagant features of the mask with large, overhanging eyebrows, and says that it will do his blushing for him.

We'll have no Cupid hoodwink'd with a scarf,
Bearing a Tartar's painted bow of lath, 5
Scaring the ladies like a crow-keeper;
Nor no without-book prologue, faintly spoke
After the prompter, for our entrance;
But, let them measure us by what they will,
We'll measure them a measure, and be gone. 10

Romeo
Give me a torch; I am not for this ambling;
Being but heavy, I will bear the light.

Mercutio
Nay, gentle Romeo, we must have you dance.

Romeo
Not I, believe me. You have dancing shoes
With nimble soles: I have a soul of lead 15
So stakes me to the ground I cannot move.

Mercutio
You are a lover; borrow Cupid's wings
And soar with them above a common bound.

Romeo
I am too sore enpiercèd with his shaft
To soar with his light feathers; and so bound 20
I cannot bound a pitch above dull woe.
Under love's heavy burden do I sink.

Mercutio
And to sink in it should you burden love;
Too great oppression for a tender thing.

Romeo
Is love a tender thing? It is too rough, 25
Too rude, too boist'rous, and it pricks like thorn.

Mercutio
If love be rough with you, be rough with love;
Prick love for pricking, and you beat love down.
Give me a case to put my visage in. [*Putting on a mask*]
A visor for a visor! What care I 30
What curious eye doth quote deformities?
Here are the beetle brows shall blush for me.

34. *betake him to his legs:* start to dance.

35. *wantons:* foolish, flippant people, of both sexes. Romeo, from the pedestal of his love-obsession, takes a rather prim view of ordinary human enjoyment.

36. The floor of Capulet's hall would be covered with rushes. Romeo is refusing to dance and says that he will be a torchbearer instead.

37-9. He is guided by a well-known traditional saying (*grandsire phrase*) which has it that the onlooker sees the best of the game.

39. The surviving texts give different versions of this line and it is not clear what Shakespeare wrote: if he wrote *done* then the meaning would seem to be that Romeo thinks that now the entertainment is at its height he should go no further.

40. *dun's the mouse:* proverbial phrase meaning 'keep quiet!': presumably the words that would be used by a constable on watch.

41. A third layer of the pun on the word *done*. The name Dun alludes to a Christmas game in which a log, representing the horse Dun. was dragged out of the mud into the house. Mercutio is suggesting that he and his companions will be able to drag Romeo out of his condition of being in love.

42. *sir-reverence:* save your reverence. Mercutio is being ironically respectful when he refers to love.

44. Romeo reminds Mercutio and the Elizabethan audience that it is not daytime but night-time. Shakespeare's audience would have watched the play in daylight and needed to be reminded of the hour.

44-5. Mercutio points out that they are wasting their torches by hanging about, as they would be by burning them by day.

46-7. He tells Romeo not to be too literal and to accept the meaning intended in his words. 'Accept the goodness of our intentions because, for every five occasions when understanding comes by that means, it comes only once through the workings of the intellect.'

48. *And:* even if.

49. Presumably Romeo is about to relate a dream which forebodes that they should not attend the ball but he does not get a chance to tell it.

52. Romeo is punning on the word *lie*.

53. *Queen Mab:* a name for the queen of the fairies. Fairies are, in English folk-lore, little creatures in human form, who possess magical powers, often used mischievously.

54. T. J. B. Spencer notes, 'Probably not the midwife who helps fairies to give birth to other fairies, but rather the one among the fairies who performs the duties of a midwife, in "delivering" the fancies of men, *the children of an idle brain*' (line 97).

55. *agate:* the stone used for signet-rings.

Benvolio
  Come, knock and enter; and no sooner in
  But every man betake him to his legs.
Romeo
  A torch for me. Let wantons, light of heart,   35
  Tickle the senseless rushes with their heels;
  For I am proverb'd with a grandsire phrase;
  I'll be a candle-holder and look on;
  The game was ne'er so fair, and I am done.
Mercutio
  Tut, dun's the mouse, the constable's own word;   40
  If thou art Dun, we'll draw thee from the mire
  Of this sir-reverence love, wherein thou stickest
  Up to the ears. Come, we burn daylight, ho!
Romeo
  Nay, that's not so.
Mercutio   I mean, sir, in delay
  We waste our lights in vain—like lights by day.   45
  Take our good meaning, for our judgment sits
  Five times in that ere once in our five wits.
Romeo
  And we mean well in going to this mask;
  But 'tis no wit to go.
Mercutio   Why, may one ask?
Romeo
  I dreamt a dream to-night.
Mercutio   And so did I.   50
Romeo
  Well, what was yours?
Mercutio   That dreamers often lie.
Romeo
  In bed asleep, while they do dream things true.
Mercutio
  O, then I see Queen Mab hath been with you.
  She is the fairies' midwife, and she comes
  In shape no bigger than an agate stone   55
  On the fore-finger of an alderman,

57. *little atomies:* tiny creatures.

59. *spinners' legs:* spiders' legs.

61. *traces:* harness.

63. *Her whip:* She has a whip of which the handle is made of cricket's bone and the lash of gossamer (i.e. a strand of spider's web). However, as crickets have an external skeleton and do not have bones, in the ordinary sense, this may refer to its scaly legs.
65-6. This refers to a superstition that lazy girls had worms in their fingers.

68. *joiner:* a craftsman who works in wood; the suggestion seems to be that coaches for the fairies were made from the empty shells of hazel-nuts dropped by squirrels or left by grubs after they had eaten the kernel.
69. *Time out o' mind:* for longer than anyone can remember.
70. *in this state:* like a state procession in which a queen rides in her state-coach.
72. *curtsies:* bows or obeisances by either sex.

75-6. The ladies' breaths smell of sweets: it is not clear why Mab should object to this and give them blisters on their lips.

78. *a suit:* a petition for favour at court.
79. *tithe-pig:* a parson was supported by a tithe, or tenth, levied upon the income of his parishioners. A tithe-pig would be a pig as part of their payment.
81. *a benefice:* a living; that is the position of a person in charge of a church such as a rector or vicar, which provides an income for the holder.

84. *breaches:* gaps smashed in the walls of besieged towns;
ambuscadoes: ambushes.
Spanish blades: swords from Spain were famous for their quality.

90. *bakes:* hardens by sticking together. The fairies were suspected of tangling up the manes of horses.
92-4. There was a belief that certain spirits had sexual intercourse with sleeping humans; Mercutio puns on the words *bear* and *carriage: bear* meaning to bear children or to bear the weight of a lover upon them,

Drawn with a team of little atomies
Athwart men's noses as they lie asleep;
Her waggon-spokes made of long spinners' legs;
The cover, of the wings of grasshoppers;　　　60
Her traces, of the smallest spider's web;
Her collars, of the moonshine's wat'ry beams;
Her whip, of cricket's bone; the lash, of film;
Her waggoner, a small grey-coated gnat,
Not half so big as a round little worm　　　65
Prick'd from the lazy finger of a maid.
Her chariot is an empty hazel-nut,
Made by the joiner squirrel or old grub,
Time out o' mind the fairies' coachmakers.
And in this state she gallops night by night　　　70
Through lovers' brains, and then they dream of love;
O'er courtiers' knees, that dream on curtsies straight;
O'er lawyers' fingers, who straight dream on fees;
O'er ladies' lips, who straight on kisses dream,
Which oft the angry Mab with blisters plagues,　　　75
Because their breaths with sweetmeats tainted are.
Sometimes she gallops o'er a courtier's nose,
And then dreams he of smelling out a suit;
And sometime comes she with a tithe-pig's tail,
Tickling a parson's nose as 'a lies asleep,　　　80
Then dreams he of another benefice.
Sometime she driveth o'er a soldier's neck,
And then dreams he of cutting foreign throats,
Of breaches, ambuscadoes, Spanish blades,
Of healths five fathoms deep; and then anon　　　85
Drums in his ear, at which he starts and wakes,
And, being thus frighted, swears a prayer or two,
And sleeps again. This is that very Mab
That plats the manes of horses in the night;
And bakes the elf-locks in foul sluttish hairs,　　　90
Which once untangled much misfortune bodes.
This is the hag, when maids lie on their backs,
That presses them and learns them first to bear,

69

[handwritten annotations]:
ODD
Is reflectn of Mercutio
Anger
Indulgence.
Resentful about idealistic love.
Strong dislike of women.
Nothing idealistic about this.
Innocent young maidens do not exist if they dream like this.

and *of good carriage* meaning walking elegantly or well able to bear the weight of a lover.

100-3. Fantasy, that is the fancy, changes its subject matter as readily as the wind changes direction. The wind is pictured as a lover who, being rejected by the *frozen...north* angrily turns around and instead woos the *dew-dropping south.*

104. *blows us from ourselves:* diverts us from our purpose, i.e. to go to the almost forgotten ball.

106-11. Romeo is apprehensive that some, as yet unknown, consequence of the night's revels may bring about his early death.
107. *hanging in the stars:* Romeo believes that his fate is hanging over him and that it is determined by the influences of the stars.

114. One of the company has a drum and they gaily strike up as they march off in a loose procession.

SCENE V

The servingmen are clearing the hall in preparation for the dance.

2. *trencher:* wooden plate. The complaint is that Potpan is not around to help clear away and do the washing-up.

Making them women of good carriage.
This is she—
Romeo   Peace, peace, Mercutio peace!   *95*
Thou talk'st of nothing.
Mercutio   True, I talk of dreams,
Which are the children of an idle brain,
Begot of nothing but vain fantasy;
Which is as thin of substance as the air,
And more inconstant than the wind, who woos   *100*
Even now the frozen bosom of the north,
And, being anger'd, puffs away from thence,
Turning his side to the dew-dropping south.
Benvolio
This wind you talk of blows us from ourselves:
Supper is done, and we shall come too late.   *105*
Romeo
I fear, too early; for my mind misgives
Some consequence, yet hanging in the stars,
Shall bitterly begin his fearful date
With this night's revels and expire the term
Of a despised life clos'd in my breast,   *110*
By some vile forfeit of untimely death.
But He that hath the steerage of my course
Direct my sail! On, lusty gentlemen.
Benvolio
Strike, drum.

        They march about the stage. Exeunt

SCENE V—*Capulet's house*

    Enter the MASKERS. SERVINGMEN *come forth with napkins*

First Servant
Where's Potpan, that he helps not to take away? He
shift a trencher! He scrape a trencher!

71

5. *join-stools:* a stool, properly made by a joiner.
court-cubbert: a movable cabinet used to display plate.

7. *marchpane:* marzipan, almond paste.
7-8. The servingman wants his girls let in by the back door.

17-18. Capulet jocularly says that he will suspect any lady who refuses
to dance of having corns.
am I come near ye now?: Am I embarrassingly near the truth?

24. *A hall, a hall!* Clear a space!

27. *this unlook'd for sport:* the presence of Romeo and his friends.

Second Servant

When good manners shall lie all in one or two men's
hands, and they unwash'd too, 'tis a foul thing.

First Servant

Away with the join-stools, remove the court-cubbert,   5
look to the plate. Good thou, save me a piece of
marchpane; and as thou loves me let the porter let in
Susan Grindstone and Nell. Antony, and Potpan!

Second Servant

Ay, boy, ready.

First Servant

You are look'd for and call'd for, ask'd for and   10
sought for, in the great chamber.

Third Servant

We cannot be here and there too. Cheerly, boys!
Be brisk a while, and the longer liver take all!

[SERVANTS *retire*]

Enter CAPULET, *with all the* GUESTS *and* GENTLE-
WOMEN *to the* MASKERS

Capulet

Welcome, gentlemen! Ladies that have their toes
Unplagu'd with corns will have a bout with you.   15
Ah ha, my mistresses! which of you all
Will now deny to dance? She that makes dainty,
She I'll swear hath corns; am I come near ye now?
Welcome, gentlemen! I have seen the day
That I have worn a visor and could tell   20
A whispering tale in a fair lady's ear,
Such as would please. 'Tis gone, 'tis gone, 'tis gone!
You are welcome, gentlemen. Come, musicians, play.
A hall, a hall! give room; and foot it, girls.

Music plays, and they dance

More light, you knaves; and turn the tables up,   25
And quench the fire, the room is grown too hot.
Ah, sirrah, this unlook'd for sport comes well.

36. *elder:* older.

38. *a ward:* a person under the care of a guardian.

39-40. *which doth enrich the hand of yonder knight?:* Juliet's beauty, as she is dancing with *yonder knight*, is thought of as exalting her companion.

48. *The measure:* the dance.

49. Romeo hopes to dance with her, or at least touch her hand in greeting.

50. Romeo, having fallen in love at first sight with Juliet, seems to recognize it as an emotion different from his infatuation for Rosaline.

52. *by his voice:* presumably Romeo has given himself away by not knowing Juliet.

54. *antic face:* Romeo's mask.

55. *to fleer:* to grimace sneeringly.

Nay, sit, nay, sit, good cousin Capulet,
For you and I are past our dancing days.
How long is't now since last yourself and I   *30*
Were in a mask?
Second Capulet   By'r Lady, thirty years.
Capulet
What, man? 'tis not so much, 'tis not so much.
'Tis since the nuptial of Lucentio,
Come Pentecost as quickly as it will,
Some five and twenty years; and then we mask'd.   *35*
Second Capulet
'Tis more, 'tis more: his son is elder, sir;
His son is thirty.
Capulet   Will you tell me that?
His son was but a ward two years ago.
Romeo [To a SERVANT]
What lady's that which doth enrich the hand
Of yonder knight?   *40*
Servant
I know not, sir.
Romeo
O, she doth teach the torches to burn bright!
It seems she hangs upon the cheek of night
As a rich jewel in an Ethiop's ear—
Beauty too rich for use, for earth too dear!   *45*
So shows a snowy dove trooping with crows
As yonder lady o'er her fellows shows.
The measure done, I'll watch her place of stand,
And, touching hers, make blessed my rude hand.
Did my heart love till now? Forswear it, sight;   *50*
For I ne'er saw true beauty till this night.
Tybalt
This, by his voice, should be a Montague.
Fetch me my rapier, boy. What, dares the slave
Come hither, cover'd with an antic face,
To fleer and scorn at our solemnity?   *55*
Now, by the stock and honour of my kin,

64. *portly:* well-mannered and dignified.

68. *disparagement:* disrespect.

70. Capulet speaks very firmly to Tybalt who we may suppose has made a gesture of disagreement. Again, Capulet is not disposed to quarrel with his unexpected guests from the other house. His attitude is in accord with ancient rules of hospitality.

72. *An ill-beseeming semblance:* an unsuitable expression.

73. *It fits:* i.e. 'my expression is appropriate. . . .'

74-9 Capulet characteristically flies into a temper when he meets with opposition.

75. *goodman boy.* Boy is always a term of insult in Elizabethan usage, *goodman* meaning 'not a gentleman' adds to the insult.

Go to: an expression of impatience.

79. *set cock-a-hoop:* encourage disorder (it originally meant 'drink immoderately').

82. *This trick may chance to scathe you:* 'This behaviour will do you no good.'

84. *Well said, my hearts!* This is spoken to some dancers as they pass by, to give the impression that he is not upset.

a princox: an impudent pup.

To strike him dead I hold it not a sin.
Capulet
  Why, how now, kinsman! Wherefore storm you so?
Tybalt
  Uncle, this is a Montague, our foe;
  A villain, that is hither come in spite   60
  To scorn at our solemnity this night.
Capulet
  Young Romeo, is it?
Tybalt   'Tis he, that villain Romeo.
Capulet
  Content thee, gentle coz, let him alone.
  'A bears him like a portly gentleman;
  And, to say truth, Verona brags of him   65
  To be a virtuous and well-govern'd youth.
  I would not for the wealth of all this town
  Here in my house do him disparagement.
  Therefore be patient, take no note of him;
  It is my will; the which if thou respect,   70
  Show a fair presence and put off these frowns,
  An ill-beseeming semblance for a feast.
Tybalt
  It fits, when such a villain is a guest.
  I'll not endure him.
Capulet   He shall be endur'd.
  What, goodman boy! I say he shall. Go to;   75
  Am I the master here or you? Go to.
  You'll not endure him! God shall mend my soul!
  You'll make a mutiny among my guests!
  You will set cock-a-hoop! You'll be the man!
Tybalt
  Why, uncle, 'tis a shame.
Capulet   Go to, go to;   80
  You are a saucy boy. Is't so, indeed?
  This trick may chance to scathe you. I know what:
  You must contrary me. Marry, 'tis time.—
  Well said, my hearts!—You are a princox; go.

85. *More light, more light!* This is spoken to some servants.
86. *Cheerly my hearts!* This is spoken to some of the guests as Capulet moves away from Tybalt.

87-8. 'The conflict between my anger and the restraint which my uncle has forced upon me makes me tremble.' Tybalt's parting remark is an ominous prophecy of the outcome of Romeo's meeting with Juliet. It echoes Romeo's previous forebodings (see Act I, Scene iv, lines 106-11).

91-104. The first conversation between Romeo and Juliet is put into the form of a sonnet ending with the word *take*. In it Romeo represents his lips as pilgrims, visiting a holy shrine, Juliet's hand; she replies in the same terms.
91. *profane:* to treat irreverently what is holy.
92. *fine:* penalty.

95. Juliet says that the touch of his hand is not rough but tender.
96. *mannerly devotion:* devout behaviour, proper to a pilgrim.

98. She, accepting the position of a saint, puts the palm of her hand against his in a *holy palmers' kiss;* that is, the kind of kiss proper to pilgrims.

100. Juliet is gently rebuking Romeo for his suggestion made in the previous line, that he should kiss her. The emphasis falls on the word *pray'r.*
101-2. Romeo, addressing her as a saint, suggests that she should let his lips do what their hands are already doing, that is pressing together; and that she should grant this prayer of his lest he should lose his faith.
103. 'Saints do not take the initiative, but do respond to prayer'; she is now inviting him to take the kiss.

104. *Then move not.* Even in the most tender passages, Shakespeare still uses puns.

107. *O trespass sweetly urg'd!* 'This is a sin for which I am given the sweetest encouragement.'

Be quiet, or—More light, more light!—For shame!   *85*
I'll make you quiet. What!—Cheerly, my hearts!
Tybalt
  Patience perforce with wilful choler meeting
  Makes my flesh tremble in their different greeting.
  I will withdraw; but this intrusion shall,
  Now seeming sweet, convert to bitt'rest gall.   *90*

Exit

Romeo [*To* JULIET]
  If I profane with my unworthiest hand
  This holy shrine, the gentle fine is this:
  My lips, two blushing pilgrims, ready stand
  To smooth that rough touch with a tender kiss.
Juliet
  Good pilgrim, you do wrong your hand too much,   *95*
  Which mannerly devotion shows in this;
  For saints have hands that pilgrims' hands do touch,
  And palm to palm is holy palmers' kiss.
Romeo
  Have not saints lips, and holy palmers too?
Juliet
  Ay, pilgrim, lips that they must use in pray'r.   *100*
Romeo
  O, then, dear saint, let lips do what hands do!
  They pray; grant thou, lest faith turn to despair.
Juliet
  Saints do not move, though grant for prayers' sake.
Romeo
  Then move not while my prayer's effect I take.
  Thus from my lips by thine my sin is purg'd.   *105*

Kissing her

Juliet
  Then have my lips the sin that they have took.
Romeo
  Sin from my lips? O trespass sweetly urg'd!

108. *You kiss by th' book!:* literally, according to the rules; she means no doubt that Romeo kisses her in a very agreeable way.

113. *withal:* with.

115. *the chinks:* money.

116. When Romeo discovers that the girl he has fallen in love with is a Capulet, he says that his life is in the hands of his enemy.

120. *a trifling foolish banquet towards:* 'light refreshments ready.'

Give me my sin again.
       Kissing her

Juliet   You kiss by th' book.

Nurse

Madam, your mother craves a word with you.

Romeo

What is her mother?

Nurse   Marry, bachelor,   *110*
Her mother is the lady of the house,
And a good lady, and a wise and virtuous.
I nurs'd her daughter that you talk'd withal.
I tell you, he that can lay hold of her
Shall have the chinks.

Romeo   Is she a Capulet?   *115*
O dear account! my life is my foe's debt.

Benvolio

Away, be gone; the sport is at the best.

Romeo

Ay, so I fear; the more is my unrest.

Capulet

Nay, gentlemen, prepare not to be gone;
We have a trifling foolish banquet towards.   *120*
Is it e'en so? Why, then I thank you all;
I thank you, honest gentlemen; good night.
More torches here! [*Exeunt* MASKERS] Come on then,
  let's to bed.
Ah, sirrah, by my fay, it waxes late;
I'll to my rest.   *125*

    Exeunt all but JULIET *and* NURSE

Juliet

Come hither, nurse. What is yond gentleman?

Nurse

The son and heir of old Tiberio.

Juliet

What's he that now is going out of door?

81

132-3. Juliet says that she will die unmarried if she cannot have Romeo for a husband.

137. Juliet is regretting that she should have fallen in love with a Montague before she knew who he was.
138. *Prodigious:* ominous.

Nurse
  Marry, that I think be young Petruchio.
Juliet
  What's he that follows there, that would not dance? *130*
Nurse
  I know not.
Juliet
  Go ask his name.—If he be married,
  My grave is like to be my wedding bed.
Nurse
  His name is Romeo, and a Montague;
  The only son of your great enemy.   *135*
Juliet
  My only love sprung from my only hate!
  Too early seen unknown, and known too late!
  Prodigious birth of love it is to me,
  That I must love a loathed enemy.
Nurse
  What's this? What's this?
Juliet   A rhyme I learnt even now *140*
  Of one I danc'd withal.[*One calls within* 'Juliet']
Nurse   Anon, anon!
  Come, let's away; the strangers all are gone.

Exeunt

1. *old desire:* refers to Romeo's infatuation for Rosaline.

2, *young affection:* refers to his new love for Juliet.
gapes: longs to, with also the notion of gasping for.
3. *That fair:* Rosaline.
4. *match'd:* compared.
5. *again:* not 'for a second time', but 'in return'.
6. Each is captivated by the other's looks.
7. *foe suppos'd.* Since Juliet is a Capulet, Romeo, a Montague, is expected to regard her as his enemy.
complain: protest his love.
8. The image is taken from fishing and indicates that despite the attraction of love for Juliet, this particular situation is beset with dangerous traps.

14. 'Lessening the difficulties of their situation by the sweetness of their meeting.'

SCENE I

2. *dull earth:* Romeo's own body.
thy centre: Juliet. The centre means the centre of the earth, believed in Shakespeare's day to be also the centre of the universe.

ACT TWO

Enter CHORUS

Now old desire doth in his death-bed lie,
And young affection gapes to be his heir;
That fair for which love groan'd for and would die,
With tender Juliet match'd, is now not fair.
Now Romeo is belov'd, and loves again,   5
Alike bewitched by the charm of looks;
But to his foe suppos'd he must complain,
And she steal love's sweet bait from fearful hooks.
Being held a foe, he may not have access
To breathe such vows as lovers use to swear;   10
And she as much in love, her means much less
To meet her new beloved any where.
But passion lends them power, time means, to meet,
Temp'ring extremities with extreme sweet.

Exit

SCENE I—*A lane by the wall of Capulet's orchard*

Enter ROMEO

Romeo

Can I go forward when my heart is here?
Turn back, dull earth, and find thy centre out.

[*He climbs the wall and leaps down within it*]

Enter BENVOLIO *with* MERCUTIO

6. *conjure:* call up a spirit through magic. Mercutio means that he will cause Romeo to appear by means of magical incantation. In calling upon Romeo, Mercutio gives him all the characteristics of the popular image of a lover: that is, he is moody, he sighs and he writes rhymes.
7. *humours:* moods.

11. *gossip:* crony.

12. *purblina:* totally blind. Cupid the archer, son of Venus, the goddess of love, is always pictured as blind.
13. *Adam Cupid:* Adam was a name given to good archers, after Adam Bell, a famous one.
14. A reference to an old ballad which tells of a king who was smitten by love for a beggar-maid; this was the handiwork of Cupid with his arrows.
16-17. Since Romeo does not appear, Mercutio pretends to think that he is dead and seeks to raise his spirit by referring to what is most sacred to him, i.e. Rosaline's body.

20. *demesnes:* regions, i.e. sexual regions. Mercutio's indecencies start here, and this is the reason for Benvolio's saying (line 22) that if Romeo could hear this he would be angry. Mercutio replies that this would not annoy him, but it would certainly make him very angry if someone else were to have sexual intercourse with Rosaline.

23-9. This speech is full of double meanings developing the humorous indecencies.
24. *To raise a spirit:* to call up one of the dead or to cause an erection.
his mistress' circle: the magic circle drawn by a conjurer, or the female genitals.
25. *Of some strange nature:* of another man.
25-6. Letting the strange spirit stay until she had used another incantation to get rid of it; or completing intercourse.
29. 'I am only trying to make him appear' or 'I am trying to get him sexually excited.'

31. *humorous:* damp.

Benvolio
Romeo! my cousin, Romeo! Romeo!
Mercutio   He is wise,
And, on my life, hath stol'n him home to bed.
Benvolio
He ran this way, and leapt this orchard wall.   *5*
Call, good Mercutio.
Mercutio   Nay, I'll conjure too.
Romeo! humours! madman! passion! lover!
Appear thou in the likeness of a sigh;
Speak but one rhyme and I am satisfied;
Cry but 'Ay me!' pronounce but 'love' and 'dove'; *10*
Speak to my gossip Venus one fair word,
One nickname for her purblind son and heir,
Young Adam Cupid, he that shot so trim
When King Cophetua lov'd the beggar-maid!
He heareth not, he stirreth not, he moveth not; *15*
The ape is dead, and I must conjure him.
I conjure thee by Rosaline's bright eyes,
By her high forehead and her scarlet lip,
By her fine foot, straight leg, and quivering thigh,
And the demesnes that there adjacent lie, *20*
That in thy likeness thou appear to us.
Benvolio
An if he hear thee, thou wilt anger him.
Mercutio
This cannot anger him: 'twould anger him
To raise a spirit in his mistress' circle
Of some strange nature, letting it there stand *25*
Till she had laid it and conjur'd it down;
That were some spite. My invocation
Is fair and honest: in his mistress' name,
I conjure only but to raise up him.
Benvolio
Come, he hath hid himself among these trees *30*
To be consorted with the humorous night:
Blind is his love, and best befits the dark.

34-8. The general sense of this passage is that Romeo, since he cannot fulfil his desire with Rosaline, will simply sit and wish that he could. This meaning is derived from the fact that *pop'rin pear* (the name comes from the place Poperinghe, in Flanders) was a crude term for the penis and *open et cetera* is a euphemism for a vulgar name of the medlar fruit, which suggests readiness for the sexual act.

36. *when they laugh alone:* suggests that young ladies would only use the vulgar term for the medlar in their joking together in private.

39. *truckle bed:* a low bed on castors.

SCENE II

From his first line, we understand that Romeo has overheard the previous conversation.

1. ' It is easy for those who have never loved to make fun of a lover.'

6. *That thou her maid:* Diana, the goddess of the moon, was also the protector of virgins, and Juliet, being a virgin, is imagined as her maid.

7-9. Romeo calls upon Juliet to cast off her virginity. He is already envisaging her as his wife.

8. *vestal livery:* virginity. The priestesses of the Roman goddess Vesta were vowed to chastity.

Mercutio

  If love be blind, love cannot hit the mark.
  Now will he sit under a medlar tree,
  And wish his mistress were that kind of fruit   *35*
  As maids call medlars when they laugh alone.
  O Romeo, that she were, O that she were
  An open et cetera, thou a pop'rin pear!
  Romeo, good night. I'll to my truckle bed;
  This field-bed is too cold for me to sleep.   *40*
  Come, shall we go?

Benvolio   Go, then; for 'tis in vain
  To seek him here that means not to be found.

Exeunt

SCENE II—*Capulet's orchard*

Enter ROMEO

Romeo

  He jests at scars that never felt a wound.

Enter JULIET *above at a window*

  But, soft! What light through yonder window breaks?
  It is the east, and Juliet is the sun.
  Arise, fair sun, and kill the envious moon,
  Who is already sick and pale with grief   *5*
  That thou her maid art far more fair than she.
  Be not her maid, since she is envious;
  Her vestal livery is but sick and green,
  And none but fools do wear it; cast it off.
  It is my lady; O, it is my love!   *10*
  O that she knew she were!
  She speaks, yet she says nothing. What of that?
  Her eye discourses; I will answer it.
  I am too bold, 'tis not to me she speaks;
  Two of the fairest stars in all the heaven,   *15*

17. *their spheres:* the positions of the stars, which were thought to be fixed in hollow transparent concentric globes.

33. *wherefore art thou Romeo?* 'Why are you a member of the Montague family?' Juliet is already aware that this will be a barrier to their love. **34-6.** She wishes that Romeo could renounce his parentage, or if that cannot be, and yet he loves her, that she could renounce her own.

39. 'What you are really like has nothing to do with the fact that you are a Montague.'

46. *owes:* owns.
47. *doff:* put off (as one takes off clothes).

Having some business, do entreat her eyes
To twinkle in their spheres till they return.
What if her eyes were there, they in her head?
The brightness of her cheek would shame those stars,
As daylight doth a lamp; her eyes in heaven   *20*
Would through the airy region stream so bright
That birds would sing, and think it were not night.
See how she leans her cheek upon her hand!
O that I were a glove upon that hand,
That I might touch that cheek!

Juliet   Ay me!

Romeo   She speaks.   *25*

O, speak again, bright angel, for thou art
As glorious to this night, being o'er my head,
As is a winged messenger of heaven
Unto the white-upturned wond'ring eyes
Of mortals that fall back to gaze on him,   *30*
When he bestrides the lazy-pacing clouds
And sails upon the bosom of the air.

Juliet

O Romeo, Romeo! wherefore art thou Romeo?
Deny thy father and refuse thy name;
Or, if thou wilt not, be but sworn my love,   *35*
And I'll no longer be a Capulet.

Romeo [*Aside*]

Shall I hear more, or shall I speak at this?

Juliet

'Tis but thy name that is my enemy;
Thou art thyself, though not a Montague.
What's Montague? It is nor hand, nor foot,   *40*
Nor arm, nor face, nor any other part
Belonging to a man. O, be some other name!
What's in a name? That which we call a rose
By any other name would smell as sweet;
So Romeo would, were he not Romeo call'd,   *45*
Retain that dear perfection which he owes
Without that title. Romeo, doff thy name;

53. *counsel:* private thoughts.

61. *if either thee dislike:* 'if either is displeasing to you.'

68. Love makes a man bold enough to attempt anything that is possible however dangerous.

72. *sweet:* affectionate, gracious.

And for thy name, which is no part of thee,
Take all myself.

Romeo   I take thee at thy word:
Call me but love, and I'll be new baptiz'd;   50
Henceforth I never will be Romeo.

Juliet
What man art thou, that, thus bescreen'd in night,
So stumblest on my counsel?

Romeo   By a name
I know not how to tell thee who I am:
My name, dear saint, is hateful to myself,   55
Because it is an enemy to thee;
Had I it written, I would tear the word.

Juliet
My ears have yet not drunk a hundred words
Of thy tongue's uttering, yet I know the sound:
Art thou not Romeo, and a Montague?   60

Romeo
Neither, fair maid, if either thee dislike.

Juliet
How cam'st thou hither, tell me, and wherefore?
The orchard walls are high and hard to climb;
And the place death, considering who thou art,
If any of my kinsmen find thee here.   65

Romeo
With love's light wings did I o'erperch these walls,
For stony limits cannot hold love out;
And what love can do, that dares love attempt.
Therefore thy kinsmen are no stop to me.

Juliet
If they do see thee, they will murder thee.   70

Romeo
Alack, there lies more peril in thine eye
Than twenty of their swords; look thou but sweet,
And I am proof against their enmity.

Juliet
I would not for the world they saw thee here.

76. *And but:* so long as.

78. *prorogued:* put off, delayed.

82-5. Romeo here uses an image that would spring naturally to the minds of the Elizabethans in an age when great voyages of exploration were taking place; he says that, though not an experienced pilot, he would undertake a voyage to the ends of the earth if Juliet were his prize.

85-106. This whole speech gives us a vivid and sympathetic picture of a young girl, very much in love, who is afraid of her behaviour being thought too *light* but who is nevertheless anxious to make her love known.

88. *Fain would I dwell on form:* 'I should like to behave in a proper lady-like fashion.'

89. *but farewell compliment!* 'but away with the restraints of formality.'

93. *Jove.* The King of the gods used various disguises in his amorous adventures.

99. *think my haviour light:* 'think my behaviour too forward.'

101. *strange:* reserved.

Romeo

 I have night's cloak to hide me from their eyes; 75
 And but thou love me, let them find me here.
 My life were better ended by their hate
 Than death prorogued wanting of thy love.

Juliet

 By whose direction found'st thou out this place?

Romeo

 By love, that first did prompt me to enquire; 80
 He lent me counsel, and I lent him eyes.
 I am no pilot; yet, wert thou as far
 As that vast shore wash'd with the farthest sea,
 I should adventure for such merchandise.

Juliet

 Thou knowest the mask of night is on my face, 85
 Else would a maiden blush bepaint my cheek
 For that which thou hast heard me speak to-night.
 Fain would I dwell on form, fain, fain deny
 What I have spoke; but farewell compliment!
 Dost thou love me? I know thou wilt say ay, 90
 And I will take thy word; yet, if thou swear'st,
 Thou mayst prove false; at lovers' perjuries
 They say Jove laughs. O gentle Romeo,
 If thou dost love, pronounce it faithfully.
 Or, if thou think'st I am too quickly won, 95
 I'll frown, and be perverse, and say thee nay,
 So thou wilt woo; but else, not for the world.
 In truth, fair Montague, I am too fond;
 And therefore thou mayst think my haviour light;
 But trust me, gentleman, I'll prove more true 100
 Than those that have more cunning to be strange.
 I should have been more strange, I must confess,
 But that thou overheard'st, ere I was ware,
 My true love's passion. Therefore pardon me,
 And not impute this yielding to light love, 105
 Which the dark night hath so discovered.

109-10. The moon is thought *inconstant* because it visibly waxes and wanes.

114. 'I am like a heathen worshipper and you are my idol.'

116-20. Is Juliet distrustful of the suddenness of their love? Or is this already a shadow of what is to come?
117. *this contract:* their vows to each other.

121-2. Their love, at present undeveloped, may become mature by their next meeting.

131. *frank:* generous.

Romeo

  Lady, by yonder blessed moon I vow,
  That tips with silver all these fruit-tree tops—

Juliet

  O, swear not by the moon, th' inconstant moon,
  That monthly changes in her circled orb,   *110*
  Lest that thy love prove likewise variable.

Romeo

  What shall I swear by?

Juliet   Do not swear at all;
  Or, if thou wilt, swear by thy gracious self,
  Which is the god of my idolatry,
  And I'll believe thee.

Romeo   If my heart's dear love—   *115*

Juliet

  Well, do not swear. Although I joy in thee,
  I have no joy of this contract to-night:
  It is too rash, too unadvis'd, too sudden;
  Too like the lightning, which doth cease to be
  Ere one can say 'It lightens'. Sweet, good night!   *120*
  This bud of love, by summer's ripening breath,
  May prove a beauteous flow'r when next we meet.
  Good night, good night! As sweet repose and rest
  Come to thy heart as that within my breast!

Romeo

  O, wilt thou leave me so unsatisfied?   *125*

Juliet

  What satisfaction canst thou have to-night?

Romeo

  Th' exchange of thy love's faithful vow for mine.

Juliet

  I gave thee mine before thou didst request it;
  And yet I would it were to give again.

Romeo

  Wouldst thou withdraw it? For what purpose, love? *130*

Juliet

  But to be frank, and give it thee again.

97

141. *substantial:* a part of real life.

143. *bent:* inclination.

147-8. The tender humility of Juliet's love, as expressed in these lines is very beautiful.

And yet I wish but for the thing I have.
My bounty is as boundless as the sea,
My <u>love as deep</u>; the more I give to thee,
The more I have, for both are infinite.   *135*

              NURSE *calls within*

I hear some noise within. Dear love, adieu!—
Anon, good nurse!—Sweet Montague, be true.
Stay but a little, I will come again.

             Exit

Romeo
  O blessed, blessed night! I am afeard,
  Being in night, all this is but a dream,   *140*
  Too flattering-sweet to be substantial.

        Re-enter JULIET *above*

Juliet
  Three words, dear Romeo, and good night indeed.
  If that thy bent of love be honourable,
  Thy purpose marriage, send me word to-morrow,
  By one that I'll procure to come to thee,   *145*
  Where and what time thou wilt perform the rite;
  And all my fortunes at thy foot I'll lay,
  And follow thee, my lord, throughout the world.
Nurse [*Within*]
  Madam!
Juliet
  I come anon.—But if thou meanest not well,   *150*
  I do beseech thee—
Nurse [*Within*]   Madam!
Juliet   By and by, I come—
  To cease thy suit, and leave me to my grief.
  To-morrow will I send.
Romeo   So thrive my soul—
Juliet
  A thousand times good night!

             Exit

159. *tassel-gentle:* Tercel is the male peregrine falcon; *gentle*, meaning noble, applies equally to the bird and to Romeo. It was a popular Elizabethan sport to tame falcons and use them for hunting other birds. Juliet wishes that she could lure Romeo back as a falconer could his falcon.
160. Because she is under the authority of her family, she has to speak to Romeo in a whisper.
161. In Greek mythology the nymph Echo lived in a cave.

Romeo

A thousand times the worse, to want thy light. *155*
Love goes toward love as school-boys from their books;
But love from love, toward school with heavy looks.

Re-enter JULIET *above*

Juliet

Hist! Romeo, hist!—O for a falc'ner's voice,
To lure this tassel-gentle back again!
Bondage is hoarse, and may not speak aloud; *160*
Else would I tear the cave where Echo lies,
And make her airy tongue more hoarse than mine
With repetition of my Romeo's name.
Romeo!

Romeo

It is my soul that calls upon my name. *165*
How silver-sweet sound lovers' tongues by night,
Like softest music to attending ears!

Juliet

Romeo!

Romeo   My dear?

Juliet   At what o'clock to-morrow
Shall I send to thee?

Romeo   By the hour of nine.

Juliet

I will not fail. 'Tis twenty years till then. *170*
I have forgot why I did call thee back.

Romeo

Let me stand here till thou remember it.

Juliet

I shall forget, to have thee still stand there,
Rememb'ring how I love thy company.

Romeo

And I'll still stay, to have thee still forget, *175*
Forgetting any other home but this.

Juliet

'Tis almost morning. I would have thee gone;

178. *a wanton's bird:* the reference is to a selfish little girl who keeps a bird on the end of a bit of string, pulling it back whenever it tries to escape.

180. *gyves:* fetters.

184. Unlike the wanton, Juliet would be in danger of killing Romeo with too much attention.

185-6. This delicate reluctance to part from one another gives us a very real and sensitive picture of two young lovers.

189. *ghostly father:* spiritual adviser.

190. *dear hap:* great good fortune.

SCENE III

Stage Direction. *Enter Friar Lawrence:* a friar is a member of one of the four orders of holy men who lived as beggars. One of his religious duties was to hear confessions (see line 55).

2. *Check'ring:* making a pattern of light and shade.

3. *fleckel'd:* dappled.

4. The Titan referred to in this line, was, according to Greek mythology, Hyperion, the sun-god; he was supposed to ride in his chariot across the sky each day.

5. *advance his burning eye:* that is, rises higher in the sky.

7. *osier cage:* a basket. The Friar is collecting herbs in order to make medicines.

8. *baleful:* evil.

9-12. This complicated passage refers to Earth as the mother of Nature; it is both Nature's grave—dead plants return to the soil—and its womb —new seeds grow out of it to replace the old. Upon the *natural bosom*

And yet no farther than a wanton's bird,
That lets it hop a little from her hand,
Like a poor prisoner in his twisted gyves,   *180*
And with a silk thread plucks it back again,
So loving-jealous of his liberty.

Romeo
I would I were thy bird.

Juliet   Sweet, so would I.
Yet I should kill thee with much cherishing.
Good night, good night! Parting is such sweet
    sorrow   *185*
That I shall say good night till it be morrow.

Exit

Romeo
Sleep dwell upon thine eyes, peace in thy breast!
Would I were sleep and peace, so sweet to rest!
Hence will I to my ghostly father's cell,
His help to crave and my dear hap to tell.   *190*

Exit

SCENE III—*Friar Lawrence's cell*

Enter FRIAR LAWRENCE *with a basket*

Friar Lawrence
The gray-ey'd morn smiles on the frowning night,
Check'ring the eastern clouds with streaks of light;
And fleckel'd darkness like a drunkard reels
From forth day's path and Titan's fiery wheels.
Now, ere the sun advance his burning eye   *5*
The day to cheer and night's dank dew to dry,
I must up-fill this osier cage of ours
With baleful weeds and precious-juiced flowers.
The earth that's nature's mother is her tomb;
What is her burying grave, that is her womb.   *10*

of the Earth—that is, on its surface—are to be found sucking *children of divers kind*—that is, plants in great variety. Many of the plants have *many virtues* or many uses—and there are none without some uses, all of them different. (It may be thought that Shakespeare's delight in playing with words here leads him into making the Friar sound tedious —or do you think the Friar is meant by Shakespeare to be rather sententious?)

15. *mickle:* great.
16. *stones:* i.e. stones of fruits such as a plum stone.

19-20. 'Nor are there any, however originally good and useful, which may not be put to evil purposes by those who misuse them.'

23-6. The Friar holds up a flower. It contains within it, he says, that which if properly used (*smelt*) as a medicine, will cheer and stimulate but which if wrongly used (*tasted*) will poison and kill.

27. *such opposed kings:* contrary powers, grace and wilful desire, comparable to medicine and poison. (Has this remark, perhaps, some relevance to the play as a whole?)
29. Both the poisonous and the medicinal forces within the flower are extremely strong; man is subject to similarly powerful forces, *rude will* (i.e. unrestrained desires) and grace (i.e. the divine influence that operates in men).
30. *canker:* caterpillar.

32. *early tongue.* Dawn is only just breaking, and the Friar is surprised that Romeo is about so early.
33. *distempered head:* troubled mind.

And from her womb children of divers kind
We sucking on her natural bosom find;
Many for many virtues excellent,
None but for some, and yet all different.
O, mickle is the powerful grace that lies   *15*
In plants, herbs, stones, and their true qualities;
For nought so vile that on the earth doth live
But to the earth some special good doth give;
Nor aught so good but, strain'd from that fair use
Revolts from true birth, stumbling on abuse: *20*
Virtue itself turns vice, being misapplied,
And vice sometime's by action dignified.
Within the infant rind of this weak flower
Poison hath residence, and medicine power;
For this, being smelt, with that part cheers each
      part;   *25*
Being tasted, slays all senses with the heart.
Two such opposed kings encamp them still
In man as well as herbs—grace and rude will;
And where the worser is predominant,
Full soon the canker death eats up that plant.   *30*

Enter ROMEO

Romeo
  Good morrow, father!
Friar Lawrence   Benedicite!
  What early tongue so sweet saluteth me?
  Young son, it argues a distempered head
  So soon to bid good morrow to thy bed.
  Care keeps his watch in every old man's eye,   *35*
  And where care lodges sleep will never lie;
  But where unbruised youth with unstuff'd brain
  Doth couch his limbs, there golden sleep doth reign.
  Therefore thy earliness doth me assure
  Thou art uprous'd with some distemp'rature;   *40*
  Or if not so, then here I hit it right—
  Our Romeo hath not been in bed to-night.

105

47. *That's my good son.* The Friar is relieved to hear that Romeo has overcome his infatuation for Rosaline—but, of course, he does not know yet about Juliet!

51-2. *both our remedies . . . lies:* 'You can heal both of us, because you are a priest.'

54. 'What I am asking for will benefit my foe as well as me.' The *foe* is, of course, Juliet.

55-6. The Friar fails to understand what Romeo is talking about—as well he may!—and tells him that an incomprehensible confession is likely to be given an incomprehensible absolution.

Romeo
  That last is true; the sweeter rest was mine.
Friar Lawrence
  God pardon sin! Wast thou with Rosaline?
Romeo
  With Rosaline, my ghostly father? No;   45
  I have forgot that name, and that name's woe.
Friar Lawrence
  That's my good son; but where hast thou been then?
Romeo
  I'll tell thee ere thou ask it me again.
  I have been feasting with mine enemy;
  Where, on a sudden, one hath wounded me   50
  That's by me wounded; both our remedies
  Within thy help and holy physic lies.
  I bear no hatred, blessed man, for, lo,
  My intercession likewise steads my foe.
Friar Lawrence
  Be plain, good son, and homely in thy drift;   55
  Riddling confession finds but riddling shrift.
Romeo
  Then plainly know my heart's dear love is set
  On the fair daughter of rich Capulet.
  As mine on hers, so hers is set on mine;
  And all combin'd, save what thou must combine   60
  By holy marriage. When, and where, and how,
  We met, we woo'd, and made exchange of vow,
  I'll tell thee as we pass; but this I pray,
  That thou consent to marry us to-day.
Friar Lawrence
  Holy Saint Francis! What a change is here!   65
  Is Rosaline, that thou didst love so dear,
  So soon forsaken? Young men's love, then, lies
  Not truly in their hearts, but in their eyes.
  Jesu Maria, what a deal of brine
  Hath wash'd thy sallow cheeks for Rosaline!   70
  How much salt water thrown away in waste,

73. Compare Act I, Scene i, lines 126-7: *With tears augmenting the fresh morning's dew, Adding to clouds more clouds with his deep sighs.* The lover's sighs are thought of as forming a small cloud of droplets, which the sun would evaporate in due course.

82. The Friar gently reminds Romeo that it is foolish infatuation he disapproves of, not love.

87-8. 'She (Rosaline) knew that your love only spoke what it had learned by heart, without really understanding what the words were. That is, Romeo only talked about love without understanding what it was.

To season love, that of it doth not taste!
The sun not yet thy sighs from heaven clears,
Thy old groans yet ring in mine ancient ears;
Lo, here upon thy cheek the stain doth sit   75
Of an old tear that is not wash'd off yet.
If e'er thou wast thyself, and these woes thine,
Thou and these woes were all for Rosaline.
And art thou chang'd? Pronounce this sentence, then:
Women may fall, when there's no strength in men.   80

Romeo

Thou chid'st me oft for loving Rosaline.

Friar Lawrence

For doting, not for loving, pupil mine.

Romeo

And bad'st me bury love.   Not in a grave
To lay one in, another out to have.

Romeo

I pray thee chide me not; her I love now   85
Doth grace for grace and love for love allow;
The other did not so.

Friar Lawrence   O, she knew well
Thy love did read by rote that could not spell.
But come, young waverer, come, go with me,
In one respect I'll thy assistant be;   90
For this alliance may so happy prove
To turn your households' rancour to pure love.

Romeo

O, let us hence; I stand on sudden haste.

Friar Lawrence

Wisely and slow; they stumble that run fast.

Exeunt

SCENE IV

11-12. Romeo's answer will be as bold as the challenge.

15. *pin:* the very centre of the target in archery (the 'bull's eye' was a piece of cloth fastened with a pin).

19. *Prince of Cats:* Tybalt was the name of a Cat Prince in a fairy-tale (pet cats are sometimes still called 'Tib').
20-1. *prick-song:* a simple melody. In this whole passage, Mercutio is making fun of Tybalt's attention to the formalities of duelling. There was at the time a cult of this kind, originating on the Continent, regarded with contempt by some Englishmen.

SCENE IV—*A street*

Enter BENVOLIO *and* MERCUTIO

Mercutio
Where the devil should this Romeo be?
Came he not home to-night?
Benvolio
Not to his father's; I spoke with his man.
Mercutio
Why, that same pale hard-hearted wench, that Rosaline,
Torments him so that he will sure run mad.   5
Benvolio
Tybalt, the kinsman to old Capulet,
Hath sent a letter to his father's house.
Mercutio
A challenge, on my life.
Benvolio
Romeo will answer it.
Mercutio
Any man that can write may answer a letter.   10
Benvolio
Nay, he will answer the letter's master, how he
dares, being dared.
Mercutio
Alas, poor Romeo, he is already dead: stabb'd with
a white wench's black eye; run through the ear with
a love-song; the very pin of his heart cleft with the   15
blind bow-boy's butt-shaft. And is he a man to en-
counter Tybalt?
Benvolio
Why, what is Tybalt?
Mercutio
More than Prince of Cats. O, he's the courageous
captain of compliments. He fights as you sing prick-   20
song: keeps time, distance, and proportion; he rests
his minim rests, one, two, and the third in your

23. *button:* that is, on his opponent's shirt; a skilful fencer was supposed to be able to touch any particular button at will. Mercutio probably favoured the more traditional form of fighting with the long-sword.
24. *the very first house:* of the highest rank.
25. *the first and second cause:* the formal taking of offence and issuing of a challenge.
passado: a lunge with foot forward.
26. *the punto reverso:* backhanded cut.
the hay! the final thrust.
28. *affecting fantasticoes:* those who put on very extravagant behaviour. People of this sort often also spoke with an affected accent and Mercutio mimics this in the next line.

33-4. *who stand so much on the new form:* who pay so much attention to the new manners (compare the modern English phrase, 'good form' meaning 'the proper way to behave'). Note also the word-play on *form* and *bench.*
35. *their bones, their bones:* pun on the French word 'bon' meaning 'good'.

37. *Without his roe:* with only half his name, therefore only half himself or looking exhausted like a fish that has spawned.
38. *numbers:* verses.
Petrarch: a famous Italian poet whose beloved was called Laura.
39. *to his lady:* compared with Rosaline; it must be remembered that Mercutio still thinks that Romeo is in love with that girl.
40-2. Mercutio goes on to jest at Romeo, imagining him thinking that a number of famous beauties, Dido, Cleopatra, Helen, Hero and Thisbe were mere nothings when compared with Rosaline.
42. *hildings and harlots:* immoral women.

46-92. The rapidity of movement and wit in the next fifty lines is most bewildering; it must have given great delight to the Elizabethan audience. The most important points are explained below.

47. *The slip, sir:* (1) as in the modern expression 'to give someone the slip'; (2) a counterfeit coin.

bosom; the very butcher of a silk button, a duellist,
a duellist; a gentleman of the very first house, of the
first and second cause. Ah, the immortal passado!   25
the punto reverso! the hay!—

Benvolio

The what?

Mercutio

The pox of such antic, lisping, affecting fantasticoes;
these new tuners of accent!—'By Jesu, a very good
blade! a very tall man! a very good whore!' Why,   30
is not this a lamentable thing, grandsire, that we
should be thus afflicted with these strange flies, these
fashion-mongers, these pardon me's, who stand so
much on the new form that they cannot sit at ease
on the old bench? O, their bones, their bones!   35

Enter ROMEO

Benvolio

Here comes Romeo, here comes Romeo.

Mercutio

Without his roe, like a dried herring. O flesh, flesh,
how art thou fishified! Now is he for the numbers
that Petrarch flow'd in; Laura, to his lady, was a kit-
chen-wench—marry, she had a better love to berhyme   40
her; Dido, a dowdy; Cleopatra, a gipsy; Helen and
Hero, hildings and harlots; Thisbe, a gray eye or so,
but not to the purpose—Signior Romeo, bon jour!
There's a French salutation to your French slop.
You gave us the counterfeit fairly last night.   45

Romeo

Good morrow to you both. What counterfeit did I
give you?

Mercutio

The slip, sir, the slip; can you not conceive?

Romeo

Pardon, good Mercutio; my business was great, and
in such a case as mine a man may strain courtesy.   50

56. *the very pink:* perfection.

59. *pump:* shoe.
flower'd: ornamented with punched holes.

64. *faints.* This is an old form of the third person plural of a verb, which was still sometimes used in Shakespeare's time.

65. *Swits and spurs . . . or I'll cry a match:* 'Keep it going, keep it going, or I'll say I've won.' (*Swits and spurs* means 'with switch (whip) and spurs'; i.e. 'flat out.')

66. *the wild-goose chase:* a frantic cross-country race in which whoever takes the lead has to be followed by the others.

68-9 *Was I with you there for the goose?* 'Did I keep up with you on the chase?' i.e. the contest of wit.

70-1. 'I have never known you in any company when you were not playing the fool.'

Mercutio

That's as much as to say, such a case as yours con-
strains a man to bow in the hams.

Romeo

Meaning, to curtsy.

Mercutio

Thou hast most kindly hit it.

Romeo

A most courteous exposition.   55

Mercutio

Nay, I am the very pink of courtesy.

Romeo

Pink for flower.

Mercutio

Right.

Romeo

Why, then is my pump well flower'd.

Mercutio

Sure wit! Follow me this jest now till thou hast worn   60
out thy pump, that, when the single sole of it is worn,
the jest may remain, after the wearing, solely singular.

Romeo

O single-sol'd jest, solely singular for the singleness!

Mercutio

Come between us, good Benvolio; my wits faints.

Romeo

Swits and spurs, swits and spurs; or I'll cry a match.   65

Mercutio

Nay, if our wits run the wild-goose chase, I am done;
for thou hast more of the wild goose in one of thy
wits than, I am sure, I have in my whole five. Was
I with you there for the goose?

Romeo

Thou wast never with me for anything when thou   70
wast not there for the goose.

Mercutio

I will bite thee by the ear for that jest.

77. *cheveril:* kid-leather. Mercutio says that Romeo is flogging the joke too far.

79-80. Far from giving up, Romeo picks up the word *broad*, and calls Mercutio *a broad goose*, i.e. a jester given to 'broad' (improper) jokes.

84. *natural:* idiot.

85. *bauble:* (1) the stick carried by a jester; (2) penis.

86. Benvolio intervenes because he sees that Mercutio is becoming wildly improper again.

87. *against the hair:* against my inclination.

88. *thy tale large:* (1) 'your story improper'; (2) 'your penis large'.

89-91. As in the previous speech, Mercutio's lines have two levels of meaning, one proper, one improper. (1) 'You are wrong: I would have made my story short, for I had come to the end of it and did not intend to continue further with the argument.' (2) 'You are wrong; I'd have made my penis small again, for I had thrust as deep as I could and meant to withdraw.'

94. *a shirt and a smock:* a man and a woman.

Romeo

Nay, good goose, bite not.

Mercutio

Thy wit is a very bitter sweeting; it is a most sharp
sauce. 75

Romeo

And is it not then well serv'd in to a sweet goose?

Mercutio

O, here's a wit of cheveril, that stretches from an inch
narrow to an ell broad!

Romeo

I stretch it out for that word 'broad', which, added
to the goose, proves thee far and wide a broad goose. 80

Mercutio

Why, is not this better now than groaning for love?
Now art thou sociable, now art thou Romeo; now art
thou what thou art by art as well as by nature; for
this drivelling love is like a great natural that runs
lolling up and down to hide his bauble in a hole. 85

Benvolio

Stop there, stop there.

Mercutio

Thou desirest me to stop in my tale against the hair.

Benvolio

Thou wouldst else have made thy tale large.

Mercutio

O, thou art deceiv'd: I would have made it short;
for I was come to the whole depth of my tale, and 90
meant, indeed, to occupy the argument no longer.

Romeo

Here's goodly gear!

Enter NURSE *and her man,* PETER

Mercutio

A sail, a sail!

Benvolio

Two, two; a shirt and a smock.

101. *God ye good den:* Mercutio corrects the Nurse and says 'Good evening'. The Elizabethans said 'Good evening' when we would say 'Good afternoon'. As soon as the Nurse arrives, Mercutio starts to poke fun at her.

104. *the prick of noon:* the very point of noon, but the word also carries its modern sexual meaning.

105. The Nurse, of course, understands Mercutio's impropriety and is properly shocked.

Nurse
  Peter!   95
Peter
  Anon.
Nurse
  My fan, Peter.
Mercutio
  Good Peter, to hide her face; for her fan's the fairer
  face.
Nurse
  God ye good morrow, gentlemen.   100
Mercutio
  God ye good den, fair gentlewoman.
Nurse
  Is it good den?
Mercutio
  'Tis no less, I tell ye; for the bawdy hand of the dial
  is now upon the prick of noon.
Nurse
  Out upon you! What a man are you?   105
Romeo
  One, gentlewoman, that God hath made himself to
  mar.
Nurse
  By my troth, it is well said. 'For himself to mar'
  quoth 'a! Gentlemen, can any of you tell me where I
  may find the young Romeo?   110
Romeo
  I can tell you; but young Romeo will be older when
  you have found him than he was when you sought
  him. I am the youngest of that name, for fault of a
  worse.
Nurse
  You say well.   115
Mercutio
  Yea, is the worst well? Very well took, i' faith; wisely,
  wisely.

119-20. Benvolio and Mercutio pretend to think that the Nurse is a prostitute inviting Romeo to her house.

120. *So ho!:* a huntsman's cry on sighting the quarry; hence Romeo's next line.

122. *hare:* (1) the game that is sighted; (2) a prostitute. Mercutio's song is an elaborate playing with the word *hare* in its double meaning, and the word *hoar* (whore) similarly.

136. *ropery:* offensive jokes.

Nurse

If you be he, sir, I desire some confidence with you.

Benvolio

She will indite him to some supper.

Mercutio

A bawd, a bawd, a bawd! So ho!   *120*

Romeo

What hast thou found?

Mercutio

No hare, sir; unless a hare, sir, in a lenten pie, that is
something stale and hoar ere it be spent.

He walks by them and sings

An old hare hoar,
And an old hare hoar,   *125*
Is very good meat in Lent;
But a hare that is hoar
Is too much for a score,
When it hoars ere it be spent.

Romeo, will you come to your father's? We'll to *130*
dinner thither.

Romeo

I will follow you.

Mercutio

Farewell, ancient lady; farewell, [*sings*] lady, lady,
lady.

Exeunt MERCUTIO *and* BENVOLIO

Nurse

I pray you, sir, what saucy merchant was this that *135*
was so full of his ropery?

Romeo

A gentleman, nurse, that loves to hear himself talk,
and will speak more in a minute than he will stand to
in a month.

Nurse

An 'a speak anything against me, I'll take him down, *140*
an 'a were lustier than he is, and twenty such Jacks;

121

143-4. *flirt-gills* and *skains-mates:* loose women.

154-5. *fool's paradise:* seduction.

169. *shrift:* confession and absolution.

and if I cannot, I'll find those that shall. Scurvy knave!
I am none of his flirt-gills; I am none of his skains-
mates. And thou must stand by too, and suffer every
knave to use me at his pleasure?   *145*

Peter

I saw no man use you at his pleasure; if I had, my
weapon should quickly have been out, I warrant you.
I dare draw as soon as another man, if I see occasion
in a good quarrel, and the law on my side.

Nurse

Now, afore God, I am so vex'd that every part about *150*
me quivers. Scurvy knave!—Pray you, sir, a word;
and as I told you, my young lady bid me enquire you
out; what she bid me say I will keep to myself. But
first let me tell ye, if ye should lead her in a fool's
paradise, as they say, it were a very gross kind of be- *155*
haviour, as they say; for the gentlewoman is young;
and, therefore, if you should deal double with her,
truly it were an ill thing to be offer'd to any gentlewoman, and very weak dealing.

Romeo

Nurse, commend me to thy lady and mistress. I pro- *160*
test unto thee—

Nurse

Good heart, and, i' faith, I will tell her as much. Lord,
Lord! she will be a joyful woman.

Romeo

What wilt thou tell her, nurse? Thou dost not mark
me.   *165*

Nurse

I will tell her, sir, that you do protest; which, as I
take it, is a gentleman-like offer.

Romeo

Bid her devise
Some means to come to shrift this afternoon;
And there she shall at Friar Lawrence' cell   *170*
Be shriv'd and married. Here is for thy pains.

177. *a tackled stair:* a rope ladder.

178. *high top-gallant:* a small extra mast fixed on the top of the main-mast in a sailing-ship.

179. *my convoy:* my conveyance.

180. *quit:* reward.

186. 'Two can keep a secret if one is done away with.'

190-1. *fain lay knife aboard:* claim her for his own, like a pirate.

191. *had as lief:* would rather.

194. *clout:* a cloth.

195. *versal:* universal.

197. *an R:* this was commonly called *the dog's name*, the sound resembling a growl.

Nurse
  No, truly, sir; not a penny.
Romeo
  Go to; I say you shall.
Nurse
  This afternoon, sir? Well, she shall be there.
Romeo
  And stay, good nurse—behind the abbey wall   *175*
  Within this hour my man shall be with thee,
  And bring thee cords made like a tackled stair;
  Which to the high top-gallant of my joy
  Must be my convoy in the secret night.
  Farewell; be trusty, and I'll quit thy pains.   *180*
  Farewell; commend me to thy mistress.
Nurse
  Now God in heaven bless thee!—
  Hark you, sir.
Romeo
  What say'st thou, my dear nurse?
Nurse
  Is your man secret? Did you ne'er hear say   *185*
  Two may keep counsel, putting one away?
Romeo
  I warrant thee my man's as true as steel.
Nurse
  Well, sir. My mistress is the sweetest lady—Lord,
  Lord! when 'twas a little prating thing! O, there is a
  nobleman in town, one Paris, that would fain lay knife *190*
  aboard; but she, good soul, had as lief see a toad, a
  very toad, as see him. I anger her sometimes, and tell
  her that Paris is the properer man; but, I'll warrant
  you, when I say so she looks as pale as any clout in
  the versal world. Doth not rosemary and Romeo *195*
  begin both with a letter?
Romeo
  Ay, nurse; what of that? Both with an R.

200. *prettiest sententious:* pretty sayings. What they were we never learn as Romeo departs having had enough of the Nurse's talk. (The Nurse probably meant 'sentences'.)

205. *Before and apace:* 'Go in front of me and quickly.'

SCENE V

6. *louring:* threatening.

7. Love here means Venus, whose chariot was drawn by swift-winged doves.

14. *bandy:* get her to him and back again quickly.

16. This line reflects one of the main themes of the play: that is, the conflict between the generations.

Nurse

    Ah, mocker! that's the dog's name. R is for the—no,
    I know it begins with some other letter. And she hath
    the prettiest sententious of it, of you and rosemary, *200*
    that it would do you good to hear it.

Romeo

    Commend me to thy lady.

Nurse

    Ay, a thousand times.—Peter!

Peter

    Anon.

Nurse [*Handing him her fan*]

    Before and apace.   *205*

                   Exeunt

SCENE V—*Capulet's orchard*

            Enter JULIET

Juliet

    The clock struck nine when I did send the nurse;
    In half an hour she promis'd to return.
    Perchance she cannot meet him—that's not so.
    O, she is lame! Love's heralds should be thoughts,
    Which ten times faster glide than the sun's beams   *5*
    Driving back shadows over louring hills;
    Therefore do nimble-pinion'd doves draw Love,
    And therefore hath the wind-swift Cupid wings.
    Now is the sun upon the highmost hill
    Of this day's journey; and from nine till twelve   *10*
    Is three long hours, yet she is not come.
    Had she affections and warm youthful blood,
    She would be as swift in motion as a ball;
    My words would bandy her to my sweet love,
    And his to me.   *15*
    But old folks—many feign as they were dead;
    Unwieldy, slow, heavy, and pale as lead.

26. *What a jaunce ... :* 'What a caper!'

38. *simple:* foolish.
38-45. In this speech, the Nurse is being deliberately ambiguous; it is to be noted that throughout this scene she is teasing Juliet by delaying.

43. *flower of courtesy:* the perfect example of a courteous man.

Enter NURSE *and* PETER

O God, she comes! O honey nurse, what news?
Hast thou met with him? Send thy man away.
Nurse
  Peter, stay at the gate. [*Exit* PETER]   20
Juliet
  Now, good sweet nurse—O Lord, why look'st thou sad?
  Though news be sad, yet tell them merrily;
  If good, thou shamest the music of sweet news
  By playing it to me with so sour a face.
Nurse
  I am aweary, give me leave a while: 25
  Fie, how my bones ache! What a jaunce have I had!
Juliet
  I would thou hadst my bones and I thy news.
  Nay, come, I pray thee speak; good, good nurse, speak.
Nurse
  Jesu, what haste? Can you not stay a while?
  Do you not see that I am out of breath?   30
Juliet
  How art thou out of breath, when thou hast breath
  To say to me that thou art out of breath?
  The excuse that thou dost make in this delay
  Is longer than the tale thou dost excuse.
  Is thy news good or bad? Answer to that;   35
  Say either, and I'll stay the circumstance.
  Let me be satisfied, is't good or bad?
Nurse
  Well, you have made a simple choice; you know not
  how to choose a man. Romeo! no, not he; though
  his face be better than any man's, yet his leg excels 40
  all men's; and for a hand, and a foot, and a body,
  though they be not to be talk'd on, yet they are past
  compare. He is not the flower of courtesy, but I'll
  warrant him as gentle as a lamb. Go thy ways,
  wench; serve God. What, have you din'd at home? 45

62. *Marry, come up:* an indignant expression.

65. *Here's such a coil!* 'What a state of things!'

70. Juliet is blushing.

Juliet

No, no. But all this did I know before.
What says he of our marriage? What of that?

Nurse

Lord, how my head aches! What a head have I!
It beats as it would fall in twenty pieces.
My back a t' other side—ah, my back, my back!   *50*
Beshrew your heart for sending me about
To catch my death with jauncing up and down!

Juliet

I' faith, I am sorry that thou art not well.
Sweet, sweet, sweet nurse, tell me, what says my love?

Nurse

Your love says like an honest gentleman, and a   *55*
courteous, and a kind, and a handsome, and, I warrant, a virtuous—Where is your mother?

Juliet

Where is my mother! Why, she is within;
Where should she be? How oddly thou repliest!
'Your love says like an honest gentleman,   *60*
Where is your mother?'

Nurse   O God's lady dear!
Are you so hot? Marry, come up, I trow;
Is this the poultice for my aching bones?
Henceforward, do your messages yourself.

Juliet

Here's such a coil! Come, what says Romeo?   *65*

Nurse

Have you got leave to go to shrift to-day?

Juliet

I have.

Nurse

Then hie you hence to Friar Lawrence' cell;
There stays a husband to make you a wife.
Now comes the wanton blood up in your cheeks;   *70*
They'll be in scarlet straight at any news.
Hie you to church; I must another way,

74. *a bird's nest:* Juliet's bedroom.

75-6. The Nurse is here indulging in the sort of crude humour that coarse-minded people still enjoy when wedding nights are mentioned.

SCENE VI

1-2. The Friar is asking for a blessing upon the marriage that he is about to celebrate. In the next two speeches, both in Romeo's defiance of death and in the Friar's warning about the possible consequences of such an all-consuming passion, we experience a foretaste of the tragedy coming on.

4. *countervail:* cancel out.

11-12. It is in the nature of the exquisite flavour of the *sweetest honey*, that it soon palls; so a too-violent love will quickly die.

To fetch a ladder, by the which your love
Must climb a bird's nest soon when it is dark.
I am the drudge, and toil in your delight;   75
But you shall bear the burden soon at night.
Go; I'll to dinner; hie you to the cell.

Juliet

Hie to high fortune! Honest nurse, farewell.

Exeunt

SCENE VI—*Friar Lawrence's cell*

Enter FRIAR LAWRENCE *and* ROMEO

Friar Lawrence

So smile the heavens upon this holy act
That after-hours with sorrow chide us not!

Romeo

Amen, amen! But come what sorrow can,
It cannot countervail the exchange of joy
That one short minute gives me in her sight.   5
Do thou but close our hands with holy words,
Then love-devouring death do what he dare;
It is enough I may but call her mine.

Friar Lawrence

These violent delights have violent ends,
And in their triumph die; like fire and powder,   10
Which, as thy kiss, consume. The sweetest honey
Is loathsome in his own deliciousness,
And in the taste confounds the appetite.
Therefore love moderately: long love doth so;
Too swift arrives as tardy as too slow.   15

Enter JULIET

Here comes the lady. O, so light a foot
Will ne'er wear out the everlasting flint.

133

18-20. 'A lover could ride upon the spider's threads that sway in the summer air and yet not fall, so empty are the pleasures of this world, of which passion is but one.'

26. *To blazon it:* to describe it fittingly.

30-1. 'A true understanding (of the happiness of their love) sets greater store by the feeling itself than the expression of it.'

32. 'Only those whose love is meagre can give an adequate summary of it.'

A lover may bestride the gossamer
That idles in the wanton summer air
And yet not fall, so light is vanity.   20

Juliet

Good even to my ghostly confessor.

Friar Lawrence

Romeo shall thank thee, daughter, for us both.

Juliet

As much to him, else is his thanks too much.

Romeo

Ah, Juliet, if the measure of thy joy
Be heap'd like mine, and that thy skill be more   25
To blazon it, then sweeten with thy breath
This neighbour air, and let rich music's tongue
Unfold the imagin'd happiness that both
Receive in either by this dear encounter.

Juliet

Conceit, more rich in matter than in words,   30
Brags of his substance, not of ornament.
They are but beggars that can count their worth;
But my true love is grown to such excess
I cannot sum up sum of half my wealth.

Friar Lawrence

Come, come with me, and we will make short work;   35
For, by your leaves, you shall not stay alone
Till holy church incorporate two in one.

Exeunt

1-4. Once again there is a sense of foreboding; Benvolio fears there may be trouble.

8. *by the operation . . . cup:* 'under the influence of two glasses of wine.'
9. *drawer:* barman.

11-13. 'Come, come, you are as hot-tempered as any man in Italy, and as quick to become angry under provocation as you are ready to be provoked.'

ACT THREE

SCENE I—*A public place*

Enter MERCUTIO, BENVOLIO, PAGE, *and* SERVANTS

Benvolio

I pray thee, good Mercutio, let's retire.
The day is hot, the Capulets abroad,
And if we meet we shall not scape a brawl;
For now, these hot days, is the mad blood stirring.

Mercutio

Thou art like one of these fellows that, when he   5
enters the confines of a tavern, claps me his sword
upon the table, and says 'God send me no need of
thee!' and by the operation of the second cup draws
him on the drawer, when, indeed, there is no need.

Benvolio

Am I like such a fellow?   10

Mercutio

Come, come, thou art as hot a Jack in thy mood as
any in Italy; and as soon moved to be moody, and as
soon moody to be moved.

Benvolio

And what to?

Mercutio

Nay, an there were two such, we should have none   15
shortly, for one would kill the other. Thou! why,
thou wilt quarrel with a man that hath a hair more or
a hair less in his beard than thou hast. Thou wilt
quarrel with a man for cracking nuts, having no other
reason but because thou hast hazel eyes. What eye   20
but such an eye would spy out such a quarrel? Thy
head is as full of quarrels as an egg is full of meat;

137

31. *fee simple:* absolute legal possession.

31-2. *of my life for an hour and a quarter:* the period for which so quarrelsome a man might expect to survive.

43. *consortest:* belong to a company of travelling minstrels. Naturally Mercutio takes such a suggestion as an insult.

44-7. Mercutio picks up this term and flings it back at Tybalt, playing with the words *discords* and *fiddlestick*.

46. *Here's my fiddlestick:* he lays his hand on his sword.

47. *Zounds:* 'God's wounds', a violent oath.

and yet thy head hath been beaten as addle as an egg
for quarrelling. Thou hast quarrell'd with a man for
coughing in the street, because he hath wakened thy   25
dog that hath lain asleep in the sun. Didst thou not
fall out with a tailor for wearing his new doublet before
Easter? With another for tying his new shoes with old
riband? And yet thou wilt tutor me from quarrelling!

Benvolio

An I were so apt to quarrel as thou art, any man   30
should buy the fee simple of my life for an hour and a
quarter.

Mercutio

The fee simple! O simple!

Enter TYBALT *and* OTHERS

Benvolio

By my head, here comes the Capulets.

Mercutio

By my heel, I care not.   35

Tybalt

Follow me close, for I will speak to them.
Gentlemen, good den; a word with one of you.

Mercutio

And but one word with one of us? Couple it with
something; make it a word and a blow.

Tybalt

You shall find me apt enough to that, sir, an you will   40
give me occasion.

Mercutio

Could you not take some occasion without giving?

Tybalt

Mercutio, thou consortest with Romeo.

Mercutio

Consort! What, dost thou make us minstrels? An
thou make minstrels of us, look to hear nothing but   45
discords. Here's my fiddlestick; here's that shall make
you dance. Zounds, consort!

55-6. Mercutio takes the word *man* to mean servant, and retorts that Romeo will only be Tybalt's follower when he goes after him to a duelling place (*field*).

61. *appertaining rage:* the anger which would normally be the natural response to such an insult. Why does Romeo, who is not a coward, refuse Tybalt's challenge?

64. *Boy:* an insult in Elizabethan times.

67. *devise:* realize. Again, what is the reason for Romeo's apparent love for Tybalt?

72. *Alla stoccata:* an Italian expression in fencing used here as a nickname for Tybalt, referring as Mercutio had done previously (Act II, Scene iv, line 2) to Tybalt's reputation as a keen fencer.

Benvolio

  We talk here in the public haunt of men;
  Either withdraw unto some private place,
  Or reason coldly of your grievances,   *50*
  Or else depart; here all eyes gaze on us.

Mercutio

  Men's eyes were made to look, and let them gaze;
  I will not budge for no man's pleasure, I.

Enter ROMEO

Tybalt

  Well, peace be with you, sir. Here comes my man.

Mercutio

  But I'll be hang'd, sir, if he wear your livery.   *55*
  Marry, go before to field, he'll be your follower;
  Your worship in that sense may call him man.

Tybalt

  Romeo, the love I bear thee can afford
  No better term than this: thou art a villain.

Romeo

  Tybalt, the reason that I have to love thee   *60*
  Doth much excuse the appertaining rage
  To such a greeting. Villain am I none;
  Therefore, farewell; I see thou know'st me not.

Tybalt

  Boy, this shall not excuse the injuries
  That thou hast done me; therefore turn and draw.   *65*

Romeo

  I do protest I never injur'd thee,
  But love thee better than thou canst devise
  Till thou shalt know the reason of my love;
  And so, good Capulet—which name I tender
  As dearly as mine own—be satisfied.   *70*

Mercutio

  O calm, dishonourable, vile submission!
  Alla stoccata carries it away. [*Draws*]
  Tybalt, you rat-catcher, will you walk?

77. *dry-beat:* beat up.
78. *pilcher:* scabbard.

81. An invitation to start the fight.

89. *a:* on.
I am sped: 'I am done for.'

Tybalt
  What wouldst thou have with me?
Mercutio
  Good King of Cats, nothing but one of your nine   75
  lives; that I mean to make bold withal, and, as you
  shall use me hereafter, dry-beat the rest of the eight.
  Will you pluck your sword out of his pilcher by the
  ears? Make haste, lest mine be about your ears ere
  it be out.   80
Tybalt
  I am for you. [*Draws*]
Romeo
  Gentle Mercutio, put thy rapier up.
Mercutio
  Come, sir, your passado. [*They fight*]
Romeo
  Draw, Benvolio; beat down their weapons.
  Gentlemen, for shame, forbear this outrage!   85
  Tybalt! Mercutio! the Prince expressly hath
  Forbid this bandying in Verona streets.
  Hold, Tybalt! Good Mercutio!

> TYBALT *under* ROMEO'S *arm thrusts* MERCUTIO *in,*
> *and flies with his friends*

Mercutio   I am hurt.
  A plague a both your houses! I am sped.
  Is he gone and hath nothing?
Benvolio   What, art thou hurt?   90
Mercutio
  Ay, ay, a scratch, a scratch; marry, 'tis enough.
  Where is my page? Go, villain, fetch a surgeon.

> *Exit* PAGE

Romeo
  Courage, man; the hurt cannot be much.
Mercutio
  No, 'tis not so deep as a well, nor so wide as a church

96. *a grave man:* even when dying, Mercutio makes a pun.

107. *near ally:* close relative.

113. Romeo speaks of himself as a sword, the hardness and resilience (*temper*) of which has been softened.

117. 'This day's misfortune casts a sense of foreboding over the days to come.'

door, but 'tis enough, 'twill serve. Ask for me to-   95
morrow, and you shall find me a grave man. I am
peppered, I warrant, for this world. A plague a both
your houses! Zounds, a dog, a rat, a mouse, a cat, to
scratch a man to death! A braggart, a rogue, a villain,
that fights by the book of arithmetic! Why the devil   100
came you between us? I was hurt under your arm.

Romeo

I thought all for the best.

Mercutio

Help me into some house, Benvolio, or I shall faint.
A plague a both your houses!
They have made worms' meat of me.   105
I have it, and soundly too—Your houses!

Exeunt MERCUTIO *and* BENVOLIO

Romeo

This gentleman, the Prince's near ally,
My very friend, hath got this mortal hurt
In my behalf; my reputation stain'd
With Tybalt's slander—Tybalt, that an hour   110
Hath been my cousin. O sweet Juliet,
Thy beauty hath made me effeminate,
And in my temper soften'd valour's steel!

Re-enter BENVOLIO

Benvolio

O Romeo, Romeo, brave Mercutio is dead!
That gallant spirit hath aspir'd the clouds,   115
Which too untimely here did scorn the earth.

Romeo

This day's black fate on moe days doth depend;
This but begins the woe others must end.

Re-enter TYBALT

Benvolio

Here comes the furious Tybalt back again.

145

121. *respective lenity: lenity* means gentleness; *respective* may refer to Romeo's respect for the Prince's order about street-fighting or to his regard for the fact that, by his marriage to Juliet, Tybalt is now his kinsman.

122. *conduct:* guide.

134. Our awareness of the intervention of Fate into the scheme of the tragedy grows with Romeo's remark.

Stage Direction. *Enter citizens.* On the printed page this seems very sudden, but on the stage the fight would last some time and people would have gathered at the sound of the disturbance.

135-6. The citizen, very responsibly in view of the Prince's order attempts to arrest Benvolio.

Romeo
  Alive in triumph and Mercutio slain!   *120*
  Away to heaven respective lenity,
  And fire-ey'd fury be my conduct now!
  Now, Tybalt, take the 'villain' back again
  That late thou gav'st me; for Mercutio's soul
  Is but a little way above our heads,   *125*
  Staying for thine to keep him company.
  Either thou or I, or both, must go with him.

Tybalt
  Thou, wretched boy, that didst consort him here,
  Shalt with him hence.

Romeo   This shall determine that.

                    They fight; TYBALT *falls*

Benvolio
  Romeo, away, be gone.   *130*
  The citizens are up, and Tybalt slain.
  Stand not amaz'd. The Prince will doom thee death
  If thou art taken. Hence, be gone, away!

Romeo
  O, I am fortune's fool!

Benvolio   Why dost thou stay?

                Exit ROMEO.   *Enter* CITIZENS

First Citizen
  Which way ran he that kill'd Mercutio?   *135*
  Tybalt, that murderer, which way ran he?

Benvolio
  There lies that Tybalt.

First Citizen   Up, sir, go with me;
  I charge thee in the Prince's name, obey.

        Enter PRINCE, *attended;* MONTAGUE, CAPULET, *their*
                    WIVES, *and all*

Prince
  Where are the vile beginners of this fray?

147

140-1. *discover all The unlucky manage of this fatal brawl:* 'tell you all about what happened in this fight.'

152. *nice:* insignificant.

155. *unruly spleen:* violent anger.

169. *entertain'd:* thought of.

Benvolio

   O noble Prince, I can discover all   *140*
   The unlucky manage of this fatal brawl:
   There lies the man, slain by young Romeo,
   That slew thy kinsman, brave Mercutio.

Lady Capulet

   Tybalt, my cousin! O my brother's child!
   O Prince! O husband! O, the blood is spill'd   *145*
   Of my dear kinsman! Prince, as thou art true,
   For blood of ours shed blood of Montague.
   O cousin, cousin!

Prince

   Benvolio, who began this bloody fray?

Benvolio

   Tybalt, here slain, whom Romeo's hand did slay;   *150*
   Romeo that spoke him fair, bid him bethink
   How nice the quarrel was, and urg'd withal
   Your high displeasure. All this, uttered
   With gentle breath, calm look, knees humbly
      bow'd
   Could not take truce with the unruly spleen   *155*
   Of Tybalt, deaf to peace, but that he tilts
   With piercing steel at bold Mercutio's breast;
   Who, all as hot, turns deadly point to point,
   And, with a martial scorn, with one hand beats
   Cold death aside, and with the other sends   *160*
   It back to Tybalt, whose dexterity
   Retorts it. Romeo he cries aloud
   'Hold, friends! friends, part!' and, swifter than his tongue,
   His agile arm beats down their fatal points,
   And 'twixt them rushes; underneath whose arm   *165*
   An envious thrust from Tybalt hit the life
   Of stout Mercutio; and then Tybalt fled;
   But by and by comes back to Romeo,
   Who had but newly entertain'd revenge,
   And to't they go like lightning; for ere I   *170*
   Could draw to part them was stout Tybalt slain;

187. *My blood:* 'one of my family', that is, Mercutio.

194. *attend our will:* this is an order to Capulet and Montague themselves to come and hear judgement and the details of the fine at Court.

And as he fell did Romeo turn and fly.
This is the truth, or let Benvolio die.

Lady Capulet

He is a kinsman to the Montague,
Affection makes him false, he speaks not true;   *175*
Some twenty of them fought in this black strife,
And all those twenty could but kill one life.
I beg for justice, which thou, Prince, must give:
Romeo slew Tybalt, Romeo must not live.   *180*

Prince

Romeo slew him; he slew Mercutio.
Who now the price of his dear blood doth owe?

Montague

Not Romeo, Prince; he was Mercutio's friend;
His fault concludes but what the law should end,
The life of Tybalt.

Prince   And for that offence,
Immediately we do exile him hence.   *185*
I have an interest in your hate's proceeding,
My blood for your rude brawls doth lie a-bleeding;
But I'll amerce you with so strong a fine
That you shall all repent the loss of mine.
I will be deaf to pleading and excuses,   *190*
Nor tears nor prayers shall purchase out abuses;
Therefore use none. Let Romeo hence in haste,
Else when he is found that hour is his last.
Bear hence this body, and attend our will:
Mercy but murders, pardoning those that kill.   *195*

Exeunt

SCENE II

In this beautiful speech, we begin to understand the fullness of Juliet's love, which seems so much more than just girlish excitement. She desires the act of love, not just for the physical pleasure, but because it represents for her the pinnacle of marriage. It is to be a supreme experience, something quite different from the subject of the Nurse's crudities. The lines are all the more moving, because we realize that the lovers will meet only to be parted again as a result of Romeo's exile.

1-2. Shakespeare again uses the mythological image of the sun as the fiery chariot of the Greek god Phœbus.

3. *Phaethon:* in Greek mythology, Phœbus' son, who one day stole the chariot and found himself unable to manage the horses in the proper fashion.

6. *runaways' eyes may wink: wink* means shut; the meaning of *runaways'* is obscure and has been much disputed. The most acceptable interpretation is 'people who would spy on lovers', or Peeping Toms.

12-13. Although Juliet will surrender herself to Romeo and both will give up their virginity (in this they will *lose*, the stakes being their *stainless maidenhoods*) she will gain a longed-for experience (*a winning match*) the consummation of their love.

14-16. 'Hide the blushes of a girl, who has never known a man sexually, with the darkness of night, until my new and unfamiliar passion is able to accept the act of love as pure and right.'

17. *thou day in night:* Romeo is the day; his presence will shine out against the darkness.

26-8. The *mansion* she has bought is Romeo; she too has been sold, to him in a mutual exchange (that is, in their marriage vows) and she sees the sexual act as a fulfilment of the contract, for which she is longing.

SCENE II—*Capulet's orchard*

Enter JULIET

Juliet

    Gallop apace, you fiery-footed steeds
    Towards Phœbus' lodging; such a waggoner
    As Phaethon would whip you to the west,
    And bring in cloudy night immediately.
    Spread thy close curtain, love-performing night,   5
    That runaways' eyes may wink, and Romeo
    Leap to these arms, untalk'd of and unseen.
    Lovers can see to do their amorous rites
    By their own beauties; or if love be blind,
    It best agrees with night. Come, civil night,   10
    Thou sober-suited matron, all in black,
    And learn me how to lose a winning match,
    Play'd for a pair of stainless maidenhoods;
    Hood my unmann'd blood, bating in my cheeks,
    With thy black mantle, till strange love, grown bold,   15
    Think true love acted simple modesty.
    Come, night; come, Romeo; come, thou day in night;
    For thou wilt lie upon the wings of night
    Whiter than new snow on a raven's back.
    Come, gentle night, come, loving black-brow'd night,   20
    Give me my Romeo; and, when he shall die,
    Take him and cut him out in little stars,
    And he will make the face of heaven so fine
    That all the world will be in love with night,
    And pay no worship to the garish sun.   25
    O, I have bought the mansion of a love,
    But not possess'd it; and though I am sold,
    Not yet enjoy'd. So tedious is this day
    As is the night before some festival
    To an impatient child that hath new robes,   30
    And may not wear them. O, here comes my nurse,

34. In this line, the irony that has been running through the speech reaches its climax, for we can guess the news that the Nurse is bringing.

37. The Nurse is as incoherent in her grief as she was in her gossip, and unwittingly misleads Juliet into thinking that Romeo is dead.

43-51. This speech is one of the most difficult for a modern audience to enter into, for in her deepest grief, Juliet indulges in a series of complicated puns. It must be realized, however, that for an Elizabethan audience there would be nothing dramatically inappropriate in this. The meaning becomes easier to understand if the word *I* in lines 45 and 46 and the third *I* in line 48 are replaced by 'Ay', meaning 'Yes'.
47. *cockatrice:* a mythological creature, hatched by a serpent from a cock's egg, supposed to kill by looking at you.

51. *weal:* happiness.

54. *corse:* corpse.

Enter NURSE *with cords*

And she brings news; and every tongue that speaks
But Romeo's name speaks heavenly eloquence.
Now, nurse, what news? What hast thou there? The cords
That Romeo bid thee fetch?

Nurse   Ay, ay, the cords.   35

Throws them down

Juliet
Ay, me! what news? Why dost thou wring thy hands?
Nurse
Ah, well-a-day! he's dead, he's dead, he's dead.
We are undone, lady, we are undone.
Alack the day! he's gone, he's kill'd, he's dead.
Juliet
Can heaven be so envious?
Nurse   Romeo can,   40
Though heaven cannot. O Romeo, Romeo!
Who ever would have thought it? Romeo!
Juliet
What devil art thou that dost torment me thus?
This torture should be roar'd in dismal hell.
Hath Romeo slain himself? Say thou but 'I'   45
And that bare vowel I shall poison more
Than the death-darting eye of cockatrice.
I am not I if there be such an 'I';
Or those eyes shut that makes thee answer 'I'.
If he be slain, say 'I'; or if not, 'No';   50
Brief sounds determine of my weal or woe.
Nurse
I saw the wound, I saw it with mine eyes—
God save the mark!—here on his manly breast.
A piteous corse, a bloody piteous corse;
Pale, pale as ashes, all bedaub'd in blood,   55
All in gore-blood. I swounded at the sight.

57. *poor bankrupt:* her heart is bankrupt because she has spent all its ove on Romeo (*bought the mansion of a love*), who is now, she thinks, dead.

59. *Vile earth:* her body. She wants to die.

67. *dreadful trumpet:* the last trumpet, which will sound when the world ends.

73-85. In this speech, Juliet, shocked by the news that Romeo has killed Tybalt, is expressing her horror that one who seemed so fine a man should be a murderer. She uses a series of paradoxes in which inward character is contrasted with outward appearance.

81. *bower:* hide in a bower, enclose.

82-3. Compare these lines with Lady Capulet's image of Paris in Act I, Scene iii, lines 83-9.

Juliet

O, break, my heart! poor bankrupt, break at once!
To prison, eyes: ne'er look on liberty.
Vile earth, to earth resign; end motion here;
And thou and Romeo press one heavy bier!　　　　60

Nurse

O Tybalt, Tybalt, the best friend I had!
O courteous Tybalt! honest gentleman!
That ever I should live to see thee dead!

Juliet

What storm is this that blows so contrary?
Is Romeo slaughter'd, and is Tybalt dead?　　　　65
My dearest cousin and my dearer lord?
Then, dreadful trumpet, sound the general doom;
For who is living if those two are gone?

Nurse

Tybalt is gone, and Romeo banished;
Romeo that kill'd him, he is banished.　　　　70

Juliet

O God! Did Romeo's hand shed Tybalt's blood?

Nurse

It did, it did; alas the day, it did!

Juliet

O serpent heart, hid with a flow'ring face!
Did ever dragon keep so fair a cave?
Beautiful tyrant! fiend angelical!　　　　75
Dove-feather'd raven! wolfish-ravening lamb!
Despised substance of divinest show!
Just opposite to what thou justly seem'st,
A damned saint, an honourable villain!
O nature, what hadst thou to do in hell,　　　　80
When thou didst bower the spirit of a fiend
In mortal paradise of such sweet flesh?
Was ever book containing such vile matter
So fairly bound? O, that deceit should dwell
In such a gorgeous palace!

Nurse　　　　　　　　　　There's no trust,　　　　85

87. *dissemblers:* deceivers.
88. *aqua vitae:* brandy or some other strong drink.

90-4. In this speech, by contrast, Juliet's love re-awakens and she scolds the Nurse for speaking ill of Romeo.

98-9. 'Who will stand up for Romeo, if I, his newly-married wife, do not?'

102-4. Juliet tells her tears to dry up, for they should signify sorrow, but hers are mistakenly falling over joyous news; that is, that Romeo is still alive.
103. *tributary:* paying a tribute.

109. *fain:* gladly.

116-120. 'If woe delights in or finds it necessary to be accompanied by other sorrows, why could not the news or Tybalt's death have been followed by the death of my father or mother, or both, which might have caused me conventional grief?'

No faith, no honesty in men; all perjur'd,
All forsworn, all naught, all dissemblers.
Ah, where's my man? Give me some aqua vitae.
These griefs, these woes, these sorrows, make me old.
Shame come to Romeo!

Juliet   Blister'd be thy tongue   *90*
For such a wish! He was not born to shame:
Upon his brow shame is asham'd to sit;
For 'tis a throne where honour may be crown'd
Sole monarch of the universal earth.
O, what a beast was I to chide at him!   *95*

Nurse
Will you speak well of him that kill'd your cousin?

Juliet
Shall I speak ill of him that is my husband?
Ah, poor my lord, what tongue shall smooth thy name,
When I, thy three-hours wife, have mangled it?
But wherefore, villain, didst thou kill my cousin?   *100*
That villain cousin would have kill'd my husband.
Back, foolish tears, back to your native spring;
Your tributary drops belong to woe,
Which you, mistaking, offer up to joy.
My husband lives that Tybalt would have slain,   *105*
And Tybalt's dead that would have slain my husband.
All this is comfort; wherefore weep I then?
Some word there was, worser than Tybalt's death,
That murder'd me; I would forget it fain,
But, O, it presses to my memory   *110*
Like damned guilty deeds to sinners' minds:
'Tybalt is dead, and Romeo banished'.
That 'banished', that one word 'banished',
Hath slain ten thousand Tybalts. Tybalt's death
Was woe enough, if it had ended there;   *115*
Or if sour woe delights in fellowship
And needly will be rank'd with other griefs,
Why followed not, when she said 'Tybalt's dead',
Thy father or thy mother, nay, or both,

121. 'But coming after Tybalt's death. . .' Are the expressions of Juliet's grief excessive?

132. *beguil'd:* fooled.

134-7. Evidently, at this point Juliet does not expect Romeo to be able to visit her at all, and fears that she will never consummate her marriage, as she has longed. She can see no life without Romeo and is resigned to die a virgin without husband.

139. *wot:* know.

Which modern lamentation might have mov'd?   *120*
But, with a rear-ward following Tybalt's death,
'Romeo is banished'—to speak that word
Is father, mother, Tybalt, Romeo, Juliet,
All slain, all dead. 'Romeo is banished'—
There is no end, no limit, measure, bound,   *125*
In that word's death; no words can that woe sound.
Where is my father and my mother, nurse?

Nurse

Weeping and wailing over Tybalt's corse.
Will you go to them? I will bring you thither.

Juliet

Wash they his wounds with tears! Mine shall be
    spent,   *130*
When theirs are dry, for Romeo's banishment.
Take up those cords. Poor ropes, you are beguil'd,
Both you and I, for Romeo is exil'd;
He made you for a highway to my bed,
But I, a maid, die maiden-widowed.   *135*
Come, cords; come, nurse; I'll to my wedding-bed;
And death, not Romeo, take my maidenhead!

Nurse

Hie to your chamber; I'll find Romeo
To comfort you. I wot well where he is.
Hark ye, your Romeo will be here at night.   *140*
I'll to him; he is hid at Lawrence' cell.

Juliet

O, find him! give this ring to my true knight,
And bid him come to take his last farewell.

Exeunt

SCENE III

1. *fearful:* full of fear.

2-3. The Friar speaks of misfortune as being in love with Romeo; and he repeats the image in speaking of Romeo being married to disaster.

4. *doom:* judgement.

9. Like Juliet, Romeo indulges in word-play at a moment of strong emotion.

SCENE III—*Friar Lawrence's cell*

Enter FRIAR LAWRENCE

Friar Lawrence
Romeo, come forth; come forth, thou fearful man;
Affliction is enamour'd of thy parts,
And thou art wedded to calamity.

Enter ROMEO

Romeo
Father, what news? What is the Prince's doom?
What sorrow craves acquaintance at my hand   5
That I yet know not?
Friar Lawrence   Too familiar
Is my dear son with such sour company;
I bring thee tidings of the Prince's doom.
Romeo
What less than doomsday is the Prince's doom?
Friar Lawrence
A gentler judgment vanish'd from his lips—   10
Not body's death, but body's banishment.
Romeo
Ha, banishment! Be merciful, say 'death';
For exile hath more terror in his look,
Much more than death. Do not say 'banishment'.
Friar Lawrence
Here from Verona art thou banished.   15
Be patient, for the world is broad and wide.
Romeo
There is no world without Verona walls,
But purgatory, torture, hell itself.
Hence banished is banish'd from the world,
And world's exile is death. Then 'banished'   20
Is death mis-term'd; calling death 'banished',

163

*All that he lives for he won't
be able to have/see so he might
as well be dead.*

26. *rush'd aside:* brushed aside.

29-51. The extraordinary violence of Romeo's grief matches that of Juliet.

39. Juliet's lips are thought of as blushing because they touch each other.

52. *fond:* foolish.

Thou cut'st my head off with a golden axe,
And smil'st upon the stroke that murders me.

Friar Lawrence

O deadly sin! O rude unthankfulness!
Thy fault our law calls death; but the kind Prince,　25
Taking thy part, hath rush'd aside the law,
And turn'd that black word death to banishment.
This is dear mercy, and thou seest it not.

Romeo

'Tis torture, and not mercy; heaven is here
Where Juliet lives, and every cat, and dog,　30
And little mouse, every unworthy thing,
Live here in heaven and may look on her;
But Romeo may not. More validity,
More honourable state, more courtship lives
In carrion flies than Romeo. They may seize　35
On the white wonder of dear Juliet's hand,
And steal immortal blessing from her lips;
Who, even in pure and vestal modesty,
Still blush, as thinking their own kisses sin;
But Romeo may not—he is banished.　40
This may flies do, when I from this must fly;
They are free men, but I am banished.
And sayest thou yet that exile is not death?
Hadst thou no poison mix'd, no sharp-ground knife,
No sudden mean of death, though ne'er so mean,　45
But 'banished' to kill me—'banished'?
O friar, the damned use that word in hell;
Howling attends it; how hast thou the heart,
Being a divine, a ghostly confessor,
A sin-absolver, and my friend profess'd,　50
To mangle me with that word 'banished'?

Friar Lawrence

Thou fond mad man, hear me a little speak.

Romeo

O, thou wilt speak again of banishment.

55. 'A philosophical outlook can make even misfortune tolerable.'

63. 'Let me discuss your situation with you.'

72-3. A far-fetched image, but possibly, in a way, appropriate to Romeo's state of distraction.

74-8. We must try to visualize this on stage: the flustered Friar is trying to persuade Romeo to hide himself, and, at the same time, is seeking to discover who is outside.

Friar Lawrence
  I'll give thee armour to keep off that word;
  Adversity's sweet milk, philosophy,   55
  To comfort thee, though thou art banished.

Romeo
  Yet 'banished'? Hang up philosophy;
  Unless philosophy can make a Juliet,
  Displant a town, reverse a prince's doom,
  It helps not, it prevails not. Talk no more.   60

Friar Lawrence
  O, then I see that madmen have no ears.

Romeo
  How should they, when that wise men have no eyes?

Friar Lawrence
  Let me dispute with thee of thy estate.

Romeo
  Thou canst not speak of that thou dost not feel.
  Wert thou as young as I, Juliet thy love,   65
  An hour but married, Tybalt murdered,
  Doting like me, and like me banished,
  Then mightst thou speak, then mightst thou tear thy
      hair,
  And fall upon the ground, as I do now,
  Taking the measure of an unmade grave.   70

            Knocking within

Friar Lawrence
  Arise; one knocks. Good Romeo, hide thyself.

Romeo
  Not I; unless the breath of heart-sick groans,
  Mist-like, enfold me from the search of eyes.

            Knocking

Friar Lawrence
  Hark how they knock! Who's there? Romeo, arise;
  Thou wilt be taken.—Stay awhile.—Stand up;   75
                      [*Knocking*]
  Run to my study.—By and by.—God's will,

85. *O woeful sympathy!* This refers to the similarity between Romeo and Juliet in their grief.

92. Apparently the Nurse, having upbraided Romeo for his behaviour, is shocked into sympathy by his grief-stricken face when he looks up at her.

98. *My conceal'd lady:* the fact that she is his lady (that is, his wife) has not yet been made known.

What simpleness is this!—I come, I come. [*Knocking*]
Who knocks so hard? Whence come you? What's your
will?

Nurse [*Within*]
Let me come in and you shall know my errand;
I come from Lady Juliet.

Friar Lawrence   Welcome, then.   80

Enter NURSE

Nurse
O holy friar, O, tell me, holy friar,
Where's my lady's lord, where's Romeo?

Friar Lawrence
There on the ground, with his own tears made drunk.

Nurse
O, he is even in my mistress' case,
Just in her case!

Friar Lawrence   O woeful sympathy!   85
Piteous predicament!

Nurse   Even so lies she,
Blubb'ring and weeping, weeping and blubb'ring.
Stand up, stand up; stand, an you be a man;
For Juliet's sake, for her sake, rise and stand;
Why should you fall into so deep an O?   90

Romeo
Nurse!

Nurse
Ah, sir! ah, sir! Well, death's the end of all.

Romeo
Spak'st thou of Juliet? How is it with her?
Doth not she think me an old murderer,
Now I have stain'd the childhood of our joy   95
With blood remov'd but little from her own?
Where is she? and how doth she? and what says
My conceal'd lady to our cancell'd love?

Nurse
O, she says nothing, sir, but weeps and weeps;

102-8. Romeo speaks of his body as though it were a house that could be destroyed. In that destruction he wishes that his name, which has caused Juliet so much grief, may be wiped out also.

115. *better temper'd:* better balanced.

122. *thy shape:* your manly form.
thy wit: your intelligence and understanding.
123. *Which:* who.
a usurer: moneylender.
122-5. Romeo is compared to a rich money-lender (*he abound'st in all*), who does not use his wealth, however, to do honour to (*bedeck*) what most deserves it, that is, his *shape*, his *love* and his *wit*.
126-7. His noble form is a mere sham (*wax*), which shows nothing of a proper valour.
128-9. His professed love is really false, and this perjury is destroying the marriage vows that he has sworn.
130-4. 'Your intelligence is misguided in the direction both of your manly vigour and your love, and like an ignorant soldier who unwittingly sets his gunpowder alight and blows himself to pieces, you destroy yourself with that part of you which should be your safeguard.' It

And now falls on her bed, and then starts up,   *100*
And Tybalt calls; and then on Romeo cries,
And then down falls again.

Romeo   As if that name,
Shot from the deadly level of a gun,
Did murder her; as that name's cursed hand
Murder'd her kinsman. O, tell me, friar, tell me,   *105*
In what vile part of this anatomy
Doth my name lodge? Tell me that I may sack
The hateful mansion.

Drawing his sword

Friar Lawrence   Hold thy desperate hand.
Art thou a man? Thy form cries out thou art:
Thy tears are womanish; thy wild acts denote   *110*
The unreasonable fury of a beast.
Unseemly woman in a seeming man!
And ill-beseeming beast in seeming both!
Thou hast amaz'd me. By my holy order,
I thought thy disposition better temper'd.   *115*
Hast thou slain Tybalt? Wilt thou slay thyself?
And slay thy lady that in thy life lives,
By doing damned hate upon thyself?
Why rail'st thou on thy birth, the heaven, and earth?
Since birth, and heaven, and earth, all three do meet *120*
In thee at once; which thou at once wouldst lose.
Fie, fie! thou sham'st thy shape, thy love, thy wit;
Which, like a usurer, abound'st in all,
And usest none in that true use indeed
Which should bedeck thy shape, thy love, thy wit.   *125*
Thy noble shape is but a form of wax,
Digressing from the valour of a man;
Thy dear love sworn but hollow perjury,
Killing that love which thou hast vow'd to cherish;
Thy wit, that ornament to shape and love,   *130*
Misshapen in the conduct of them both,
Like powder in a skilless soldier's flask,

171

should be remembered that the whole of this speech, up to this point, is a rebuke to Romeo for trying to kill himself. In the remainder of it, the Friar turns from rebuke to encouragement and gives Romeo the reasons for faith and hope.

151. *blaze:* make known.

Is set afire by thine own ignorance,
And thou dismember'd with thine own defence.
What, rouse thee, man! Thy Juliet is alive,   135
For whose dear sake thou wast but lately dead;
There art thou happy. Tybalt would kill thee,
But thou slewest Tybalt; there art thou happy too.
The law, that threaten'd death, becomes thy friend,
And turns it to exile; there art thou happy.   140
A pack of blessings lights upon thy back;
Happiness courts thee in her best array;
But, like a misbehav'd and sullen wench,
Thou pout'st upon thy fortune and thy love.
Take heed, take heed, for such die miserable.   145
Go, get thee to thy love, as was decreed,
Ascend her chamber, hence and comfort her.
But look thou stay not till the watch be set,
For then thou canst not pass to Mantua,
Where thou shalt live till we can find a time   150
To blaze your marriage, reconcile your friends,
Beg pardon of the Prince, and call thee back
With twenty hundred thousand times more joy
Than thou went'st forth in lamentation.
Go before, nurse; commend me to thy lady;   155
And bid her hasten all the house to bed,
Which heavy sorrow makes them apt unto;
Romeo is coming.
Nurse
O Lord, I could have stay'd here all the night
To hear good counsel; O, what learning is!   160
My lord, I'll tell my lady you will come.
Romeo
Do so, and bid my sweet prepare to chide.
Nurse
Here, sir, a ring she bid me give you, sir.
Hie you, make haste, for it grows very late.

Exit

166. *here stands all your state:* 'this is what you must do.'

1-2. Capulet is explaining that, because of Tybalt's death (*Things have fall'n out, sir. so unluckily*), he has had no opportunity to approach Juliet about the proposed marriage with Paris.

11. *mew'd up to her heaviness:* she has shut herself away in her grief. Lady Capulet, of course, supposes this grief to be caused by the death of Tybalt; the audience knows that it is for the banishment of her husband, Romeo.

12-13. *make a desperate tender Of my child's love:* 'risk a bold offer to you of my daughter's love'—he is relying on the probability that Juliet will obey her father's wishes as to whom she marries.

Romeo

How well my comfort is reviv'd by this!   *165*

Friar Lawrence

Go hence; good night; and here stands all your state:
Either be gone before the watch be set,
Or by the break of day disguis'd from hence.
Sojourn in Mantua; I'll find out your man,
And he shall signify from time to time   *170*
Every good hap to you that chances here.
Give me thy hand. 'Tis late; farewell; good night.

Romeo

But that a joy past joy calls out on me,
It were a grief so brief to part with thee.
Farewell.   *175*

Exeunt

SCENE IV—*Capulet's house*

Enter CAPULET, LADY CAPULET, *and* PARIS

Capulet

Things have fall'n out, sir, so unluckily
That we have had no time to move our daughter.
Look you, she lov'd her kinsman Tybalt dearly,
And so did I. Well, we were born to die.
'Tis very late; she'll not come down to-night.   *5*
I promise you, but for your company,
I would have been abed an hour ago.

Paris

These times of woe afford no time to woo.
Madam, good night; commend me to your daughter.

Lady Capulet

I will, and know her mind early to-morrow;   *10*
To-night she's mew'd up to her heaviness.

Capulet

Sir Paris, I will make a desperate tender
Of my child's love. I think she will be rul'd

22. The questions are addressed to Paris.

23. *we'll keep no great ado:* 'we won't have a showy wedding.'

30. *a Thursday:* on Thursday.

SCENE V

In Shakespeare's theatre, this scene, taking place on the upper stage, would have started as soon as Capulet moved off the main platform—emphasizing that even at the moment that Capulet was arranging a marriage for her, Juliet, already married, was with her husband just above his head.

1-2. Evidently the song of the lark has aroused Romeo to the fact that he must be away from Verona before full daylight. Juliet touchingly tries to keep him a little longer by pretending it is a nightingale that he hears.

In all respects by me; nay, more, I doubt it not.
Wife, go you to her ere you go to bed;   *15*
Acquaint her here of my son Paris' love
And bid her, mark you me, on Wednesday next—
But, soft! what day is this?

Paris   Monday, my lord.

Capulet
Monday! ha, ha! Well, Wednesday is too soon.
A Thursday let it be; a Thursday, tell her,   *20*
She shall be married to this noble earl.
Will you be ready? Do you like this haste?
We'll keep no great ado—a friend or two;
For, hark you, Tybalt being slain so late,
It may be thought we held him carelessly,   *25*
Being our kinsman, if we revel much;
Therefore we'll have some half a dozen friends,
And there an end. But what say you to Thursday?

Paris
My lord, I would that Thursday were to-morrow.

Capulet
Well, get you gone; a Thursday be it then.   *30*
Go you to Juliet ere you go to bed;
Prepare her, wife, against this wedding-day.
Farewell, my lord. Light to my chamber, ho!
Afore me, it is so very very late
That we may call it early by and by.   *35*
Good night.

                    Exeunt

SCENE V—*Capulet's orchard*

                Enter ROMEO *and* JULIET, *aloft*

Juliet
Wilt thou be gone? It is not yet near day;
It was the nightingale, and not the lark,
That pierc'd the fearful hollow of thine ear;

7. *envious streaks:* the first light of dawn, called *envious* because it is summoning him to go, as though envious of his joy with Juliet.

9. *jocund:* cheerful.

13. *meteor.* Any luminous appearance in the sky was given the name; such things were thought to originate in the sun.

17-35. As soon as Romeo says he'll gladly stay and die for it, if Juliet wants him to, she in her turn becomes anxious for him, and urges him away.

20. 'the lingering light of the moon.' Cynthia (Diana) was the goddess of the moon (*reflex* = reflection).

23. *care:* desire.

28. *sharps:* shrill notes.

29-30. *division . . . divideth:* another pun—*division* here means melody.

32. Juliet seems to be regretting the beauty of the lark's song, saying that, since it is what is driving Romeo away, it would be more agreeable if it sounded like the ugly croaking of a toad.

33. *affray:* frighten.

34. *hunts-up:* music played to rouse prospective hunters in the morning.

Nightly she sings on yond pomegranate tree.
Believe me, love, it was the nightingale.   5

Romeo

It was the lark, the herald of the morn,
No nightingale. Look, love, what envious streaks
Do lace the severing clouds in yonder east;
Night's candles are burnt out, and jocund day
Stands tiptoe on the misty mountain tops.   10
I must be gone and live, or stay and die.

Juliet

Yond light is not daylight; I know it, I:
It is some meteor that the sun exhales
To be to thee this night a torch-bearer,
And light thee on thy way to Mantua;   15
Therefore stay yet; thou need'st not to be gone.

Romeo

Let me be ta'en, let me be put to death;
I am content, so thou wilt have it so.
I'll say yon grey is not the morning's eye,
'Tis but the pale reflex of Cynthia's brow;   20
Nor that is not the lark whose notes do beat
The vaulty heaven so high above our heads.
I have more care to stay than will to go.
Come death, and welcome! Juliet wills it so.
How is't, my soul? Let's talk—it is not day.   25

Juliet

It is, it is; hie hence, be gone, away!
It is the lark that sings so out of tune,
Straining harsh discords and unpleasing sharps.
Some say the lark makes sweet division;
This doth not so, for she divideth us.   30
Some say the lark and loathed toad change eyes;
O, now I would they had chang'd voices too!
Since arm from arm that voice doth us affray,
Hunting thee hence with hunts-up to the day.
O, now be gone! More light and light it grows.   35

43. For Juliet, Romeo is everything—master, husband and lover.

54. *an ill-divining soul:* 'to divine' means to see into the future—Juliet has a premonition of disaster—another of the many reminders that the young lovers are fated to a tragic end. This vision is a particularly accurate one.

Romeo

More light and light—more dark and dark our woes!

Enter NURSE

[handwritten: The lighter it gets the darker here troubles seen.]

Nurse

Madam!

Juliet

Nurse?

Nurse

Your lady mother is coming to your chamber.
The day is broke; be wary, look about.   40

Exit

Juliet

Then, window, let day in and let life out.

Romeo

Farewell, farewell! One kiss, and I'll descend.

He goeth down

Juliet

Art thou gone so, love—lord, ay, husband, friend!
I must hear from thee every day in the hour,
For in a minute there are many days;   45
O, by this count I shall be much in years
Ere I again behold my Romeo!

Romeo

Farewell!
I will omit no opportunity
That may convey my greetings, love, to thee.   50

Juliet

O, think'st thou we shall ever meet again?

Romeo

I doubt it not; and all these woes shall serve
For sweet discourses in our times to come.

Juliet

O God, I have an ill-divining soul!
Methinks I see thee, now thou art below,   55

[handwritten: She fears he will die.]

59. Their misery at parting drains the blood from their faces.

60-4. 'Fortune is known to be changeable; why then does it have anything to do with Romeo, who is renowned for being steadfast and unchangeable? But let Fortune be changeable; for if Romeo's luck changes, he will be able to come back.'

73. *wit:* good sense.

74. *feeling loss:* a loss deeply felt.

As one dead in the bottom of a tomb;
Either my eyesight fails or thou look'st pale.

Romeo

And trust me, love, in my eye so do you;
Dry sorrow drinks our blood. Adieu, adieu!

Exit below

Juliet

O Fortune, Fortune! all men call thee fickle.   60
If thou art fickle, what dost thou with him
That is renown'd for faith? Be fickle, Fortune;
For then, I hope, thou wilt not keep him long,
But send him back.

Lady Capulet [*Within*] Ho, daughter! are you up?

Juliet

Who is't that calls? It is my lady mother.   65
Is she not down so late, or up so early?
What unaccustom'd cause procures her hither?

Enter LADY CAPULET

Lady Capulet

Why, how now, Juliet!

Juliet   Madam, I am not well.

Lady Capulet

Evermore weeping for your cousin's death?
What, wilt thou wash him from his grave with tears? 70
An if thou couldst, thou couldst not make him live;
Therefore have done. Some grief shows much of love;
But much of grief shows still some want of wit.

Juliet

Yet let me weep for such a feeling loss.

Lady Capulet

So shall you feel the loss, but not the friend   75
Which you weep for.

Juliet   Feeling so the loss,
I cannot choose but ever weep the friend.

183

81. 'Villain is a name that cannot possibly be given to Romeo.'

89. *runagate:* runaway.

97. *temper it:* mix it. Juliet presumably takes her mother's promise to have Romeo poisoned (*give him such an unaccustom'd dram*) seriously and plans to have a hand in mixing the poison, so that she can make it harmless.

101-2. In this conversation, much of what Juliet says has quite a different meaning from that which Lady Capulet supposes it to have and the audience, of course, realizes this. Consider, for example, what Juliet actually means in line 85 and in lines 99-100, and what her mother thinks she means.

Lady Capulet
  Well, girl, thou weep'st not so much for his death
  As that the villain lives which slaughter'd him.
Juliet
  What villain, madam?
Lady Capulet   That same villain, Romeo.   *80*
Juliet [*Aside*]
  Villain and he be many miles asunder!—
  God pardon him! I do, with all my heart;
  And yet no man like he doth grieve my heart.
Lady Capulet
  That is because the traitor murderer lives.
Juliet
  Ay, madam, from the reach of these my hands.   *85*
  Would none but I might venge my cousin's death!
Lady Capulet
  We will have vengeance for it, fear thou not;
  Then weep no more. I'll send to one in Mantua—
  Where that same banish'd runagate doth live—
  Shall give him such an unaccustom'd dram   *90*
  That he shall soon keep Tybalt company;
  And then I hope thou wilt be satisfied.
Juliet
  Indeed I never shall be satisfied
  With Romeo till I behold him—dead—
  Is my poor heart so for a kinsman vex'd.   *95*
  Madam, if you could find out but a man
  To bear a poison, I would temper it,
  That Romeo should, upon receipt thereof,
  Soon sleep in quiet. O, how my heart abhors
  To hear him nam'd, and cannot come to him,   *100*
  To wreak the love I bore my cousin Tybalt
  Upon his body that hath slaughter'd him!
Lady Capulet
  Find thou the means, and I'll find such a man.
  But now I'll tell thee joyful tidings, girl.

129. *a conduit:* a water-pipe.

131. *a bark:* a ship.

Juliet
    And joy comes well in such a needy time.   *105*
    What are they, beseech your ladyship?
Lady Capulet
    Well, well, thou hast a careful father, child;
    One who, to put thee from thy heaviness,
    Hath sorted out a sudden day of joy
    That thou expects not, nor I look'd not for.   *110*
Juliet
    Madam, in happy time, what day is that?
Lady Capulet
    Marry, my child, early next Thursday morn
    The gallant, young, and noble gentleman,
    The County Paris, at Saint Peter's Church,
    Shall happily make thee there a joyful bride.   *115*
Juliet
    Now, by Saint Peter's Church, and Peter too,
    He shall not make me there a joyful bride.
    I wonder at this haste, that I must wed
    Ere he that should be husband comes to woo.
    I pray you tell my lord and father, madam,   *120*
    I will not marry yet; and when I do, I swear
    It shall be Romeo, whom you know I hate,
    Rather than Paris. These are news indeed!
Lady Capulet
    Here comes your father; tell him so yourself,
    And see how he will take it at your hands.   *125*

        Enter CAPULET *and* NURSE

Capulet
    When the sun sets, the air doth drizzle dew;
    But for the sunset of my brother's son
    It rains downright.
    How now! a conduit, girl? What, still in tears?
    Evermore show'ring? In one little body   *130*
    Thou counterfeit'st a bark, a sea, a wind;
    For still thy eyes, which I may call the sea,

138. *our decree:* that is, the decision that she is to marry Paris on the following Thursday.

146-8. Juliet tries to avoid making her father angry by saying that she is grateful for the trouble he has taken, though she cannot be proud of the man he has chosen.

149. *chopt logic:* clever talk.

151. *minion:* saucy creature.

153. *fettle your fine joints:* get yourself ready. The words also convey the idea that Juliet thinks much too much of herself.

155. *hurdle:* a wooden frame on which traitors were dragged through the streets.

156. *green-sickness carrion: green-sickness* was the name given to an illness common to young women (anaemia) which made them look pale, and *carrion* is dead meat. Juliet is no doubt pale with anxiety—*tallow face* in line 157 refers to this also.

157. Lady Capulet is evidently shocked by the violence of Capulet's insulting language to their daughter.

Do ebb and flow with tears. The bark thy body is,
Sailing in this salt flood; the winds thy sighs,
Who, raging with thy tears, and they with them,   *135*
Without a sudden calm will overset
Thy tempest-tossed body. How now, wife!
Have you delivered to her our decree?

Lady Capulet

Ay, sir; but she will none, she gives you thanks.
I would the fool were married to her grave!   *140*

Capulet

Soft! take me with you, take me with you, wife.
How will she none? Doth she not give us thanks?
Is she not proud? Doth she not count her blest,
Unworthy as she is, that we have wrought
So worthy a gentleman to be her bridegroom?   *145*

Juliet

Not proud you have, but thankful that you have.
Proud can I never be of what I hate,
But thankful even for hate that is meant love.

Capulet

How how, how how, chopt logic! What is this?
'Proud'—and 'I thank you'—and 'I thank you not'—   *150*
And yet 'not proud'? Mistress minion, you,
Thank me no thankings, nor proud me no prouds,
But fettle your fine joints 'gainst Thursday next,
To go with Paris to Saint Peter's Church,
Or I will drag thee on a hurdle thither.   *155*
Out, you green-sickness carrion! Out, you baggage!
You tallow-face!

Lady Capulet   Fie, fie! what, are you mad?

Juliet

Good father, I beseech you on my knees,
Hear me with patience but to speak a word.

Capulet

Hang thee, young baggage! disobedient wretch!   *160*
I tell thee what—get thee to church a Thursday,
Or never after look me in the face.

168. *hilding:* a worthless girl.

168-9. As on previous occasions, the Nurse stands up for Juliet sturdily.

171. *smatter with your gossips, go:* 'Oh! go away and chatter with the other old women.'

172. *O, God-i-goden!* literally 'Oh! Good evening to you'. Capulet is beside himself with anger and is trying to dismiss the Nurse.

181. *of fair demesnes:* owning a fine estate.

183. 'As suitable a man as one could possibly want.'

185. *mammet:* doll.
in her fortune's tender: in the face of what fortune offers her.

188. *I'll pardon you:* meaning, of course, with threatening sarcasm, 'I'll show you the kind of pardon you'll get!'

Speak not, reply not, do not answer me;
My fingers itch. Wife, we scarce thought us blest
That God had lent us but this only child;   *165*
But now I see this one is one too much,
And that we have a curse in having her.
Out on her, hilding!
Nurse   God in heaven bless her!
You are to blame, my lord, to rate her so.
Capulet
And why, my Lady Wisdom? Hold your tongue,   *170*
Good Prudence; smatter with your gossips, go.
Nurse
I speak no treason.
Capulet   O, God-i-goden!
Nurse
May not one speak?
Capulet   Peace, you mumbling fool!
Utter your gravity o'er a gossip's bowl,
For here we need it not.
Lady Capulet   You are too hot.   *175*
Capulet
God's bread! it makes me mad:
Day, night, hour, tide, time, work, play,
Alone, in company, still my care hath been
To have her match'd; and having now provided
A gentleman of noble parentage,   *180*
Of fair demesnes, youthful, and nobly train'd,
Stuff'd, as they say, with honourable parts,
Proportion'd as one's thought would wish a man—
And then to have a wretched puling fool,
A whining mammet, in her fortune's tender,   *185*
To answer, 'I'll not wed, I cannot love,
I am too young, I pray you pardon me'!
But, an you will not wed, I'll pardon you.
Graze where you will, you shall not house with me.
Look to't, think on't; I do not use to jest.   *190*
Thursday is near; lay hand on heart, advise:

196. *I'll not be forsworn:* 'I won't be made to go back on my word'—that is, his promise to Paris that he could marry Juliet.

204. Lady Capulet's last word is exactly what one would expect from her: 'Do what you like; I wash my hands of you.'

206. *my faith in heaven:* 'I have made a vow which is recorded in heaven'—that is, her marriage vow to Romeo.

207-9. Juliet says she could only be released from her marriage vow by the death of her husband.

210-11. She cries out in misery that heaven should play such tricks upon one as defenceless as herself.

214. *and all the world to nothing:* the odds of a bet; the Nurse is saying that it is as certain as anything can be that Romeo will not return. **215.** *to challenge you:* to lay claim to. The Nurse's worldly advice is characteristic of her base outlook; she is quite incapable of appreciating the love of Romeo and Juliet, but within her obvious limits, she is well-meaning.

If you don't do as I say

An you be mine, I'll give you to my friend;
An you be not, hang, beg, starve, die in the streets,
For, by my soul, I'll ne'er acknowledge thee,
Nor what is mine shall never do thee good.   195
Trust to't, bethink you, I'll not be forsworn.

Exit

Juliet

Is there no pity sitting in the clouds
That sees into the bottom of my grief?
O, sweet my mother, cast me not away!
Delay this marriage for a month, a week;   200
Or, if you do not, make the bridal bed
In that dim monument where Tybalt lies.

Lady Capulet

Talk not to me, for I'll not speak a word;
Do as thou wilt, for I have done with thee.

Exit

Juliet

O God!—O nurse! how shall this be prevented?   205
My husband is on earth, my faith in heaven;
How shall that faith return again to earth,
Unless that husband send it me from heaven
By leaving earth? Comfort me, counsel me.
Alack, alack, that heaven should practise stratagems   210
Upon so soft a subject as myself!
What say'st thou! Hast thou not a word of joy?
Some comfort, nurse.

So why not marry another.

Nurse   Faith, here it is:
Romeo is banished; and all the world to nothing
That he dares ne'er come back to challenge you;   215
Or, if he do, it needs must be by stealth.
Then, since the case so stands as now it doth,
I think it best you married with the County.
O, he's a lovely gentleman!
Romeo's a dishclout to him; an eagle, madam,   220
Hath not so green, so quick, so fair an eye

228. *beshrew:* curse. Juliet's muttered *Amen* in line 229 is an angry endorsement of the Nurse's suggested curse upon herself.

231-4. Juliet, aware now that even the Nurse is against her, quickly pretends to accept her advice.

236. *Ancient damnation:* 'damnable old woman.'

As Paris hath. Beshrew my very heart,
I think you are happy in this second match,
For it excels your first; or, if it did not,
Your first is dead, or 'twere as good he were   225
As living here and you no use of him.

Juliet

Speak'st thou from thy heart?

are you lying.

Nurse

And from my soul too, else beshrew them both.

Juliet

Amen!

no she is not lying.

Nurse

What?   230

Juliet

Well, thou hast comforted me marvellous much.
Go in; and tell my lady I am gone,
Having displeas'd my father, to Lawrence' cell
To make confession, and to be absolv'd.

Nurse

Marry, I will; and this is wisely done.   235

Exit

Juliet

Ancient damnation! O most wicked fiend!
Is it more sin to wish me thus forsworn,
Or to dispraise my lord with that same tongue
Which she hath prais'd him with above compare
So many thousand times? Go, counsellor;   240
Thou and my bosom henceforth shall be twain.
I'll to the friar to know his remedy;
If all else fail, myself have power to die.

Exit

3. 'I certainly don't want to check his haste.'

5. The Friar says that a marriage in which the lady has had no opportunity to express an opinion is irregular.

9-14. Paris says that Capulet considers it dangerous for Juliet to brood so much upon her grief in solitude, which, however, may be easily forgotten in his company. (Of course, Capulet has said nothing of the sort!)

16. What is it that the Friar knows?

18-43. Throughout this interchange, Juliet's replies are cautious and ambiguous to avoid either committing herself to Paris or disclosing the reason why she cannot marry him.

ACT FOUR

SCENE I—*Friar Lawrence's cell*

Enter FRIAR LAWRENCE *and* COUNTY PARIS

Friar Lawrence
  On Thursday, sir? The time is very short.
Paris
  My father, Capulet will have it so,
  And I am nothing slow to slack his haste.
Friar Lawrence
  You say you do not know the lady's mind;
  Uneven is the course; I like it not.   5
Paris
  Immoderately she weeps for Tybalt's death,
  And therefore have I little talk'd of love;
  For Venus smiles not in a house of tears.
  Now, sir, her father counts it dangerous
  That she do give her sorrow so much sway,   10
  And in his wisdom hastes our marriage,
  To stop the inundation of her tears;
  Which, too much minded by herself alone,
  May be put from her by society.
  Now do you know the reason of his haste.   15
Friar Lawrence [*Aside*]
  I would I knew not why it should be slow'd.—
  Look, sir, here comes the lady toward my cell.

Enter JULIET

Paris
  Happily met, my lady and my wife!
Juliet
  That may be, sir, when I may be a wife.

27-8. Complimentary remarks made about someone who is not present are worth more than what may be just flattery.

34. *to my face:* Shakespeare is playing with words again—the meanings are (1) about my face, (2) openly.

Paris
  That may be must be, love, on Thursday next.   *20*
Juliet
  What must be shall be.
Friar Lawrence   That's a certain text.
Paris
  Come you to make confession to this father?
Juliet
  To answer that, I should confess to you.
Paris
  Do not deny to him that you love me.
Juliet
  I will confess to you that I love him.   *25*
Paris
  So will ye, I am sure, that you love me.
Juliet
  If I do so, it will be of more price
  Being spoke behind your back than to your face.
Paris
  Poor soul, thy face is much abus'd with tears.
Juliet
  The tears have got small victory by that,   *30*
  For it was bad enough before their spite.
Paris
  Thou wrong'st it more than tears with that report.
Juliet
  That is no slander, sir, which is a truth;
  And what I spake, I spake it to my face.
Paris
  Thy face is mine, and thou hast slander'd it.   *35*
Juliet
  It may be so, for it is not mine own.
  Are you at leisure, holy father, now,
  Or shall I come to you at evening mass?
Friar Lawrence
  My leisure serves me, pensive daughter, now.
  My lord, we must entreat the time alone.   *40*

41. *God shield I should disturb devotion:* 'God forbid that I should interfere with your devotions.'

48. *prorogue:* delay.

54. *presently:* immediately.

56-7. 'Before this hand will be ready to put the seal to another document.'
deed: legal contract.

59. *both:* that is, hand and heart.

64. *the commission of thy years and art:* the authority belonging to your age and wisdom. We must imagine a long pause between lines 65 and 66, during which Juliet stands, dagger in hand, whilst the Friar thinks what to do.
66-7. *I long to die ... remedy:* 'I am more than willing to die, if you can suggest no way out of the difficulty.'

Paris

　God shield I should disturb devotion!
　Juliet, on Thursday early will I rouse ye;
　Till then, adieu, and keep this holy kiss.

Exit

Juliet

　O, shut the door, and when thou hast done so,
　Come weep with me—past hope, past cure, past
　　help.　　　　　　　　　　　　　　　　　　*45*

Friar Lawrence

　O, Juliet, I already know thy grief;
　It strains me past the compass of my wits.
　I hear thou must, and nothing may prorogue it,
　On Thursday next be married to this County.

Juliet

　Tell me not, friar, that thou hear'st of this,　　*50*
　Unless thou tell me how I may prevent it;
　If, in thy wisdom, thou canst give no help,
　Do thou but call my resolution wise,
　And with this knife I'll help it presently.
　God join'd my heart and Romeo's, thou our hands;　*55*
　And ere this hand, by thee to Romeo's seal'd,
　Shall be the label to another deed,
　Or my true heart with treacherous revolt
　Turn to another, this shall slay them both.
　Therefore, out of thy long-experienc'd time,　　*60*
　Give me some present counsel; or, behold,
　'Twixt my extremes and me this bloody knife
　Shall play the umpire, arbitrating that
　Which the commission of thy years and art
　Could to no issue of true honour bring.　　　　*65*
　Be not so long to speak; I long to die,
　If what thou speak'st speak not of remedy.

Friar Lawrence

　Hold, daughter; I do spy a kind of hope,

69-70. 'which requires a course of action as dangerous as the outcome we want to avoid.'

75. *That:* (you) who.

79. *thievish ways:* streets full of thieves.

81 *charnel house:* a store-house for human bones.

83. *reeky shanks:* rotting legbones.
chapless skulls: skulls from which the jawbones have fallen.

96. *humour:* fluid.

97. *his native progress:* its natural beat.
surcease: stop.

100. *eyes' windows:* eyelids.

102. *supple government:* power of movement.

Which craves as desperate an execution
As that is desperate which we would prevent.   70
If, rather than to marry County Paris,
Thou hast the strength of will to slay thyself,
Then is it likely thou wilt undertake
A thing like death to chide away this shame,
That cop'st with death himself to scape from it;   75
And, if thou dar'st, I'll give thee remedy.

Juliet

O, bid me leap, rather than marry Paris,
From off the battlements of any tower,
Or walk in thievish ways, or bid me lurk
Where serpents are; chain me with roaring bears,   80
Or hide me nightly in a charnel house,
O'er-cover'd quite with dead men's rattling bones,
With reeky shanks and yellow chapless skulls;
Or bid me go into a new-made grave,
And hide me with a dead man in his shroud—   85
Things that, to hear them told, have made me tremble—
And I will do it without fear or doubt,
To live an unstain'd wife to my sweet love.

Friar Lawrence

Hold, then; go home, be merry, give consent
To marry Paris. Wednesday is to-morrow;   90
To-morrow night look that thou lie alone,
Let not the nurse lie with thee in thy chamber.
Take thou this vial, being then in bed,
And this distilled liquor drink thou off;
When presently through all thy veins shall run   95
A cold and drowsy humour; for no pulse
Shall keep his native progress, but surcease;
No warmth, no breath, shall testify thou livest;
The roses in thy lips and cheeks shall fade
To paly ashes, thy eyes' windows fall,   100
Like death when he shuts up the day of life;
Each part, depriv'd of supple government,
Shall, stiff and stark and cold, appear like death;

110. *bier:* the stand on which a coffin, or dead body, is conveyed.

113. *against thou shalt awake:* in preparation for the time when you will awake.
114. *drift:* plan.

119. *inconstant toy:* frivolous change of mind.

SCENE II

2. *cunning:* skilful.

And in this borrow'd likeness of shrunk death
Thou shalt continue two and forty hours,   *105*
And then awake as from a pleasant sleep.
Now, when the bridegroom in the morning comes
To rouse thee from thy bed, there art thou dead.
Then, as the manner of our country is,
In thy best robes, uncovered on the bier,   *110*
Thou shalt be borne to that same ancient vault
Where all the kindred of the Capulets lie.
In the meantime, against thou shalt awake,
Shall Romeo by my letters know our drift,
And hither shall he come; and he and I   *115*
Will watch thy waking, and that very night
Shall Romeo bear thee hence to Mantua.
And this shall free thee from this present shame,
If no inconstant toy nor womanish fear
Abate thy valour in the acting it.   *120*

Juliet

Give me, give me! O, tell not me of fear!

Friar Lawrence

Hold; get you gone, be strong and prosperous
In this resolve. I'll send a friar with speed
To Mantua, with my letters to thy lord.

Juliet

Love give me strength! and strength shall help afford. *125*
Farewell, dear father!

                Exeunt

SCENE II—*Capulet's house*

    Enter CAPULET, LADY CAPULET, NURSE, *and two or*
            three SERVINGMEN

Capulet

So many guests invite as here are writ.

            Exit a SERVINGMAN

Sirrah, go hire me twenty cunning cooks.

3-9. The Servingman is making fun with the proverb that says that it is a poor cook that will not *lick his own fingers*, that is, taste his own food.

10. 'We haven t enough provisions in stock for an occasion like this.'

14. *harlotry:* an insulting term for a girl—'silly creature.'

15. *shrift:* confession.

19. *behests:* commands.

24. *knot knit up:* marriage completed.

Servingman

　You shall have none ill, sir; for I'll try if they can lick
　their fingers.

Capulet

　How canst thou try them so?　　　　　　　　　　5

Servingman

　Marry, sir, 'tis an ill cook that cannot lick his own
　fingers; therefore he that cannot lick his fingers goes
　not with me.

Capulet

　Go, be gone.

Exit second SERVINGMAN

　We shall be much unfurnish'd for this time.　　　　10
　What, is my daughter gone to Friar Lawrence?

Nurse

　Ay, forsooth.

Capulet

　Well, he may chance to do some good on her:
　A peevish self-will'd harlotry it is.

Enter Juliet

Nurse

　See where she comes from shrift with merry look.　　15

Capulet

　How now, my headstrong! Where have you been
　　　gadding?

Juliet

　Where I have learnt me to repent the sin
　Of disobedient opposition
　To you and your behests; and am enjoin'd
　By holy Lawrence to fall prostrate here,　　　　20
　To beg your pardon. Pardon, I beseech you.
　Henceforward I am ever rul'd by you.

Capulet

　Send for the County; go tell him of this.
　I'll have this knot knit up to-morrow morning.

26. *becomed:* suitable.

28. *stand up:* Juliet has evidently knelt dutifully to her father.

31-2. Characteristically, as soon as the Friar has taken a course of action which is, Capulet supposes, convenient to himself (Capulet), he is full of the old man's praises.

36, 38-9. It should be noted that Capulet has brought the marriage forward a day and that Lady Capulet is protesting that this will not give them sufficient time for preparations.

43. *I'll play the huswife for this once:* Capulet declares that he will see to the business of getting in provisions himself; now that he has got his own way, he is all good humour.
44. *They are all forth:* Capulet has called for servants, (*What ho!*), but apparently they are all out on errands.

Juliet

    I met the youthful lord at Lawrence' cell,   25

    And gave him what becomed love I might,

    Not stepping o'er the bounds of modesty.

Capulet

    Why, I am glad on't; this is well—stand up—

    This is as't should be. Let me see the County;

    Ay, marry, go, I say, and fetch him hither.   30

    Now, afore God, this reverend holy friar,

    All our whole city is much bound to him.

Juliet

    Nurse, will you go with me into my closet

    To help me sort such needful ornaments

    As you think fit to furnish me to-morrow?   35

Lady Capulet

    No, not till Thursday; there is time enough.

Capulet

    Go, nurse, go with her. We'll to church to-morrow.

Exeunt JULIET *and* NURSE

Lady Capulet

    We shall be short in our provision;

    'Tis now near night.

Capulet   Tush, I will stir about,

    And all things shall be well, I warrant thee, wife.   40

    Go thou to Juliet, help to deck up her;

    I'll not to bed to-night; let me alone.

    I'll play the huswife for this once. What, ho!

    They are all forth; well, I will walk myself

    To County Paris, to prepare up him   45

    Against to-morrow. My heart is wondrous light

    Since this same wayward girl is so reclaim'd.

Exeunt

3. *orisons:* prayers.

4. *state:* spiritual condition.

5. *cross:* perverse. Juliet is pretending to confess that her obstinacy to her parents is sinful.

7. *cull'd:* collected.

8. *As are behoveful:* as are needed.
state: ceremonies, i.e. the wedding.

14. Juliet is about to take the Friar's potion, which will send her into a deep sleep; she expects that she will then be taken from the tomb by Romeo and not see her parents again.

15. *faint cold fear:* a terror that makes Juliet feel faint and uneasy.

23. *this:* the dagger. What does Juliet mean by '*This shall forbid it*'?

SCENE III—*Juliet's chamber*

Enter JULIET *and* NURSE

Juliet
  Ay, those attires are best; but, gentle nurse,
  I pray thee, leave me to myself to-night,
  For I have need of many orisons
  To move the heavens to smile upon my state,
  Which well thou know'st is cross and full of sin.   *5*

Enter LADY CAPULET

Lady Capulet
  What, are you busy, ho? Need you my help?
Juliet
  No, madam; we have cull'd such necessaries
  As are behoveful for our state to-morrow.
  So please you, let me now be left alone,
  And let the nurse this night sit up with you;   *10*
  For I am sure you have your hands full all
  In this so sudden business.
Lady Capulet   Good night.
  Get thee to bed, and rest; for thou hast need.

Exeunt LADY CAPULET *and* NURSE

Juliet
  Farewell! God knows when we shall meet again.
  I have a faint cold fear thrills through my veins,   *15*
  That almost freezes up the heat of life;
  I'll call them back again to comfort me.
  Nurse!—What should she do here?
  My dismal scene I needs must act alone.
  Come, vial.   *20*
  What if this mixture do not work at all?
  Shall I be married, then, to-morrow morning?
  No, no; this shall forbid it. Lie thou there.

Laying down her dagger

29. 'He has always proved a holy man.'

37. *conceit:* thoughts.
38. Juliet's terror is reflected in the way the sentence breaks up.

42. *green in earth:* only recently buried.

47. *mandrakes:* the mandrake is a poisonous plant which, because it has a forked root, is thought to resemble the human body: it was fabled to shriek when pulled out of the earth. However, Juliet is presumably imagining these shrieks to be uttered by the spirits.
49. *distraught:* driven mad.
50. *Environed:* surrounded.

57. *Stay, Tybalt, stay:* Juliet rises from her bed and holds out her hands to ward off this apparition. The whole speech is a very convincing picture of Juliet's midnight terror.

What if it be a poison which the friar
Subtly hath minister'd to have me dead,   25
Lest in this marriage he should be dishonour'd,
Because he married me before to Romeo?
I fear it is; and yet methinks it should not,
For he hath still been tried a holy man.
How, if, when I am laid into the tomb,   30
I wake before the time that Romeo
Come to redeem me? There's a fearful point.
Shall I not then be stifled in the vault,
To whose foul mouth no healthsome air breathes in,
And there die strangled ere my Romeo comes?   35
Or, if I live, is it not very like
The horrible conceit of death and night,
Together with the terror of the place—
As in a vault, an ancient receptacle
Where for this many hundred years the bones   40
Of all my buried ancestors are pack'd;
Where bloody Tybalt, yet but green in earth,
Lies fest'ring in his shroud; where, as they say,
At some hours in the night spirits resort—
Alack, alack, is it not like that I,   45
So early waking—what with loathsome smells,
And shrieks like mandrakes' torn out of the earth,
That living mortals, hearing them, run mad—
O, if I wake, shall I not be distraught,
Environed with all these hideous fears,   50
And madly play with my forefathers' joints,
And pluck the mangled Tybalt from his shroud,
And, in this rage, with some great kinsman's bone,
As with a club, dash out my desp'rate brains?
O, look! methinks I see my cousin's ghost   55
Seeking out Romeo, that did spit his body
Upon a rapier's point. Stay, Tybalt, stay.
Romeo, I come. This do I drink to thee.

She drinks and falls upon her bed within the curtains

SCENE IV

The action is continuous; no sooner has Juliet fallen on her bed within the curtains, than Lady Capulet reappears on the lower stage bustling about the wedding preparations. Evidently, the household has been up all night.

2. *the pastry:* the part of the kitchen where pastries were made.

4. *The curfew bell.* This can certainly not carry its normal meaning of an evening bell, in this context; perhaps it was a bell rung in the morning to show that the period of curfew (during which household fires had to be put out) was over.
5. *good Angelica:* so that is what the Nurse is called!
6. *cot-quean:* a man who does woman's work. This is a notable example of the Nurse's frankness, and it shows how much licence she is given.
8. *watching:* staying up all night.

11. *a mouse-hunt:* one who chases after women, particularly at night.
12. 'I'll see you don't get up to any of those games now.'

13. 'You're jealous, that's what it is.' This jocular exchange is in contrast to his behaviour to the women earlier on.

SCENE IV—*Capulet's house*

Enter LADY CAPULET *and* NURSE

Lady Capulet
  Hold, take these keys, and fetch more spices, nurse.
Nurse
  They call for dates and quinces in the pastry.

Enter CAPULET

Capulet
  Come, stir, stir, stir! The second cock hath crow'd,
  The curfew bell hath rung, 'tis three o'clock.
  Look to the bak'd meats, good Angelica;   5
  Spare not for cost.
Nurse   Go, you cot-quean, go,
  Get you to bed; faith, you'll be sick to-morrow
  For this night's watching.
Capulet
  No, not a whit; what! I have watch'd ere now
  All night for lesser cause, and ne'er been sick.   10
Lady Capulet
  Ay, you have been a mouse-hunt in your time;
  But I will watch you from such watching now.

Exeunt LADY CAPULET *and* NURSE

Capulet
  A jealous-hood, a jealous-hood!

Enter three or four SERVINGMEN *with spits
and logs and baskets*

                    Now, fellow,
  What is there?
First Fellow
  Things for the cook, sir; but I know not what.   15

215

18-19. *I have a head, sir. . . matter.* The servingman explains that he has enough commonsense to find logs without Peter's help.

20. *a merry whoreson, ha!* Capulet's modern counterpart might say, 'He's a cheerful bastard!'
21. *Thou shalt be logger-head:* Capulet puns on this remark, quipping that he has a wooden-head or blockhead.

SCENE V

4-5. *You take your pennyworths now. Sleep for a week:* 'You get some sound sleep now (because you'll get very little when Paris is with you).

6. *hath set up his rest:* an image from jousting; to have a lance at rest to have it in readiness; of course, there are bawdy overtones of an erection.

Capulet
    Make haste, make haste. [*Exit* FIRST FELLOW]
                                        Sirrah, fetch drier logs;
    Call Peter; he will show thee where they are.
Second Fellow
    I have a head, sir, that will find out logs,
    And never trouble Peter for the matter.
Capulet
    Mass, and well said; a merry whoreson, ha!   *20*
    Thou shalt be logger-head. [*Exit* SECOND FELLOW]
                                        Good faith, 'tis day;
    The County will be here with music straight,
    For so he said he would. [*Play music*] I hear him near.
    Nurse! Wife! What, ho! What, nurse, I say!

                    Re-enter NURSE

    Go waken Juliet, go and trim her up;   *25*
    I'll go and chat with Paris. Hie, make haste,
    Make haste. The bridegroom he is come already
    Make haste, I say.

                        Exeunt

SCENE V—*Juliet's chamber*

                    Enter NURSE

Nurse
    Mistress! What, mistress! Juliet! Fast, I warrant her, she.
    Why, lamb! Why, lady! Fie, you slug-a-bed!
    Why, love, I say! madam! sweetheart! Why, bride!
    What, not a word? You take your pennyworths now.
    Sleep for a week; for the next night, I warrant,   *5*
    The County Paris hath set up his rest
    That you shall rest but little. God forgive me!
    Marry, and amen. How sound is she asleep!
    I needs must wake her. Madam, madam, madam!

                        217

14-64. This very long-winded expression of grief in formal verse is perhaps the most unconvincing part of the play for a modern audience.

Ay, let the County take you in your bed;   *10*
He'll fright you up, i' faith. Will it not be?

Draws the curtains

What, dress'd, and in your clothes, and down again!
I must needs wake you. Lady! lady! lady!
Alas, alas! Help, help! my lady's dead!
O well-a-day that ever I was born!   *15*
Some aqua-vitæ, ho! My lord! My lady!

Enter LADY CAPULET

Lady Capulet
  What noise is here?
Nurse   O lamentable day!
Lady Capulet
  What is the matter?
Nurse   Look, look! O heavy day!
Lady Capulet
  O me, O me! My child, my only life,
  Revive, look up, or I will die with thee!   *20*
  Help, help! Call help.

Enter CAPULET

Capulet
  For shame, bring Juliet forth; her lord is come.
Nurse
  She's dead, deceas'd, she's dead; alack the day!
Lady Capulet
  Alack the day, she's dead, she's dead, she's dead!
Capulet
  Ha! let me see her. Out, alas! she's cold;   *25*
  Her blood is settled, and her joints are stiff.
  Life and these lips have long been separated.
  Death lies on her like an untimely frost
  Upon the sweetest flower of all the field.
Nurse
  O lamentable day!
Lady Capulet   O woeful time!   *30*

219

35-7. The idea of Death as a young girl's lover is a very widespread one in folk-tales and in art.

44-5. 'This is the most miserable hour that time, in its eternal progress onward, has ever revealed.'

Capulet
  Death, that hath ta'en her hence to make me wail,
  Ties up my tongue and will not let me speak.

Enter FRIAR LAWRENCE *and* COUNTY PARIS, *with* MUSICIANS

Friar Lawrence
  Come, is the bride ready to go to church?
Capulet
  Ready to go, but never to return.
  O son, the night before thy wedding day   *35*
  Hath Death lain with thy wife. There she lies,
  Flower as she was, deflowered by him.
  Death is my son-in-law, Death is my heir;
  My daughter he hath wedded; I will die,
  And leave him all; life, living, all is Death's.   *40*
Paris
  Have I thought long to see this morning's face,
  And doth it give me such a sight as this?
Lady Capulet
  Accurs'd, unhappy, wretched, hateful day!
  Most miserable hour that e'er time saw
  In lasting labour of his pilgrimage!   *45*
  But one, poor one, one poor and loving child,
  But one thing to rejoice and solace in,
  And cruel Death hath catch'd it from my sight!
Nurse
  O woe! O woeful, woeful, woeful day!
  Most lamentable day, most woeful day   *50*
  That ever, ever, I did yet behold!
  O day! O day! O day! O hateful day!
  Never was seen so black a day as this.
  O woeful day, O woeful day!
Paris
  Beguil'd, divorced, wronged, spited, slain!   *55*
  Most detestable Death, by thee beguil'd,
  By cruel cruel thee quite overthrown!
  O love! O life!—not life, but love in death!

70. Juliet's soul is in heaven (*his* = Death's).

71. *promotion:* her social advancement (by a good marriage).

80-1. This, of course, is an essential part of the Friar's plan.

82-3. 'Our foolish human nature makes us grieve for her death, although reason laughs at our laments, knowing the absurdity of tears when she has gone to heaven.'

84-90. This speech, in contrast to the previous lamentations, is quite moving. There is here a control of expression and emotion and it is touching that the celebrations, which we have seen in preparation, must now be changed for the funeral.

Capulet
  Despis'd, distressed, hated, martyr'd, kill'd!—
  Uncomfortable time, why cam'st thou now   60
  To murder, murder our solemnity?
  O child! O child! my soul, and not my child!
  Dead art thou; alack, my child is dead,
  And with my child my joys are buried.

Friar Lawrence
  Peace, ho, for shame! Confusion's cure lives not   65
  In these confusions. Heaven and yourself
  Had part in this fair maid; now heaven hath all,
  And all the better is it for the maid.
  Your part in her you could not keep from death,
  But heaven keeps his part in eternal life.   70
  The most you sought was her promotion,
  For 'twas your heaven she should be advanc'd;
  And weep ye now, seeing she is advanc'd
  Above the clouds, as high as heaven itself?
  O, in this love, you love your child so ill   75
  That you run mad, seeing that she is well.
  She's not well married that lives married long,
  But she's best married that dies married young.
  Dry up your tears, and stick your rosemary
  On this fair corse, and, as the custom is,   80
  In all her best array bear her to church;
  For though fond nature bids us all lament,
  Yet nature's tears are reason's merriment.

Capulet
  All things that we ordained festival
  Turn from their office to black funeral: 85
  Our instruments to melancholy bells,
  Our wedding cheer to a sad burial feast,
  Our solemn hymns to sullen dirges change;
  Our bridal flowers serve for a buried corse;
  And all things change them to the contrary.   90

Friar Lawrence
  Sir, go you in; and, madam, go with him;

94. *lour upon you for some ill:* 'frown upon you for some offence you
have committed.'
95. Is it possible to approve of the Friar's deceit and his moralizing
here?

99. *the case may be amended:* a pun. In the previous line the word means
'a state of affairs'; here the Musician presumably means a cover for
his instrument.

104. *dump:* mournful melody.

224

And go, Sir Paris. Every one prepare
To follow this fair corse unto her grave.
The heavens do lour upon you for some ill;
Move them no more by crossing their high will.   *95*

Exeunt all but NURSE *and* MUSICIANS

First Musician
  Faith, we may put up our pipes and be gone.
Nurse
  Honest good fellows, ah, put up, put up;
  For well you know this is a pitiful case.

Exit

First Musician
  Ay, by my troth, the case may be amended.

Enter PETER

Peter
  Musicians, O, musicians, 'Heart's ease,' 'Heart's *100*
  ease'! O, an you will have me live, play 'Heart's ease'.
First Musician
  Why 'Heart's ease'?
Peter
  O, musicians, because my heart itself plays 'My
  heart is full of woe'. O, play me some merry dump to
  comfort me.   *105*
First Musician
  Not a dump we! 'Tis no time to play now.
Peter
  You will not, then?
First Musician
  No.
Peter
  I will then give it you soundly.
First Musician
  What will you give us?   *110*

225

111. *gleek:* a jibe.

111-12. *give you the minstrel:* 'call you a minstrel.' Minstrel was a term of abuse: see Act III, Scene I, line 44.

115. *carry:* put up with.
crotchets: (1) in music the name of a note of a particular length, (2) insults.

117. *you note us:* another pun. Peter used the word to mean 'understand'; the Musician means 'set us to music'.

118. *put up:* put away.
put out: display.

119. *dry-beat:* beat soundly.

122-4. The words of a well-known song of the time.

129. *sound for silver:* i.e. play for money.

132. *I cry you mercy:* I beg your pardon.

Peter

No money, on my faith, but the gleek. I will give you the minstrel.

First Musician

Then will I give you the serving-creature.

Peter

Then will I lay the serving-creature's dagger on your pate. I will carry no crotchets: I'll re you, I'll fa you; 115 do you note me?

First Musician

An you re us and fa us, you note us.

Second Musician

Pray you put up your dagger, and put out your wit.

Peter

Then have at you with my wit! I will dry-beat you with an iron wit, and put up my iron dagger. Answer me 120 like men.

     'When griping grief the heart doth wound
       And doleful dumps the mind oppress,
       Then music with her silver sound'—

Why 'silver sound'? Why 'music with her silver 125 sound'? What say you, Simon Catling?

First Musician

Marry, sir, because silver hath a sweet sound.

Peter

Pretty! What say you, Hugh Rebeck?

Second Musician

I say 'silver sound' because musicians sound for silver.

Peter

Pretty too! What say you, James Soundpost? 130

Third Musician

Faith, I know not what to say.

Peter

O, I cry you mercy, you are the singer; I will say for you. It is 'music with her silver sound' because musicians have no gold for sounding.

'Then music with her silver sound   *135*
With speedy help doth lend redress.'

Exit

First Musician

What a pestilent knave is this same!

Second Musician

Hang him, Jack! Come, we'll in here; tarry for the
mourners, and stay dinner.

Exeunt

1-2. Previously Romeo has had premonitions of doom, but now, as the lovers' deaths draw close, ironically he is having joyous dreams.
2. *presage:* forecast.
3. *bosom's lord:* i.e. his heart.

10-11. Romeo is saying that if his dreams of Juliet are so delightful, how much more wonderful it will be to be actually with her.

12-15. Romeo's stream of questions indicates his eagerness for news.

17. Balthasar's reply, echoing Romeo's words, is at first ambiguous; he considers that she is *well* because, although dead, her soul is in heaven. He puts it like this to break the shock of the news.

21. *took post:* hired a horse.

24. There is a pause before Romeo speaks, as he gathers the full horror of Balthasar's message.
Then I defy you, stars: Romeo, in an outburst of passion, violently defies fate and the influence of the stars, which would separate him from Juliet.

ACT FIVE

SCENE I—*Mantua. A street*

Enter ROMEO

Romeo
  If I may trust the flattering truth of sleep,
  My dreams presage some joyful news at hand.
  My bosom's lord sits lightly in his throne,
  And all this day an unaccustom'd spirit
  Lifts me above the ground with cheerful thoughts.   *5*
  I dreamt my lady came and found me dead—
  Strange dream, that gives a dead man leave to think—!
  And breath'd such life with kisses in my lips
  That I reviv'd, and was an emperor.
  Ah me! how sweet is love itself possess'd,   *10*
  When but love's shadows are so rich in joy!

Enter BALTHASAR, *Romeo's man*

  News from Verona! How now, Balthasar!
  Dost thou not bring me letters from the friar?
  How doth my lady? Is my father well?
  How fares my Juliet? That I ask again,   *15*
  For nothing can be ill if she be well.
Balthasar
  Then she is well, and nothing can be ill.
  Her body sleeps in Capels' monument,
  And her immortal part with angels lives.
  I saw her laid low in her kindred's vault,   *20*
  And presently took post to tell it you.
  O, pardon me for bringing these ill news,
  Since you did leave it for my office, sir.
Romeo
  Is it e'en so? Then I defy you, stars.

27-9. The frenzy of Romeo's manner makes Balthasar fear that he will do something rash.

34. *I will lie with thee to-night.* He will at least lie with her in death, he says with bitter irony.

37. *an apothecary:* one who prepared medicines.

38. *which:* whom.

38-52. Romeo's description of the apothecary and his shop sets a suitable nightmarish atmosphere for the final stages of the story.

39. *weeds:* clothes.

overwhelming: overhanging.

40. *Culling of simples:* gathering herbs.

Meagre: gaunt.

45. *account:* collection.

47. *old cakes of roses:* compressed rose petals which were used for perfume.

51. *present:* immediate. The sale of poisons was a capital offence in Mantua.

52. *caitiff:* miserable.

Thou knowest my lodging: get me ink and paper,   *25*
And hire post-horses; I will hence to-night.
Balthasar
  I do beseech you, sir, have patience;
  Your looks are pale and wild, and do import
  Some misadventure.
Romeo   Tush, thou art deceiv'd;
  Leave me, and do the thing I bid thee do.   *30*
  Hast thou no letters to me from the friar?
Balthasar
  No, my good lord.
Romeo   No matter; get thee gone,
  And hire those horses; I'll be with thee straight.

Exit BALTHASAR

Well, Juliet, I will lie with thee to-night.
Let's see for means. O mischief, thou art swift   *35*
To enter in the thoughts of desperate men!
I do remember an apothecary,
And hereabouts 'a dwells, which late I noted
In tatter'd weeds, with overwhelming brows,
Culling of simples. Meagre were his looks;   *40*
Sharp misery had worn him to the bones;
And in his needy shop a tortoise hung,
An alligator stuff'd, and other skins
Of ill-shap'd fishes; and about his shelves
A beggarly account of empty boxes,   *45*
Green earthen pots, bladders, and musty seeds,
Remnants of packthread, and old cakes of roses,
Were thinly scatter'd, to make up a show.
Noting this penury, to myself I said
'An if a man did need a poison now,   *50*
Whose sale is present death in Mantua,
Here lives a caitiff wretch would sell it him.'
O, this same thought did but forerun my need;
And this same needy man must sell it me.
As I remember, this should be the house   *55*

63-5. This image is meant to suggest very sudden death: 'That life may leave my body as suddenly as the shot from a cannon.'

67. *utters:* sells.

69-71. The language here is very compressed—Romeo says that the apothecary's physical condition bears witness to his poverty and distress.

75. 'Because of my poverty, I am forced against my will to agree.' Since it cannot be supposed that the apothecary carries poison on him, he presumably goes back into his shop to get it.

Being holiday, the beggar's shop is shut.
What, ho! Apothecary!

Enter APOTHECARY

Apothecary   Who calls so loud?
Romeo
    Come hither, man. I see that thou art poor.
    Hold, there is forty ducats; let me have
    A dram of poison, such soon-speeding gear   *60*
    As will disperse itself through all the veins
    That the life-weary taker may fall dead,
    And that the trunk may be discharg'd of breath
    As violently as hasty powder fir'd
    Doth hurry from the fatal cannon's womb.   *65*
Apothecary
    Such mortal drugs I have; but Mantua's law
    Is death to any he that utters them.
Romeo
    Art thou so bare and full of wretchedness
    And fear'st to die? Famine is in thy cheeks,
    Need and oppression starveth in thy eyes,   *70*
    Contempt and beggary hangs upon thy back,
    The world is not thy friend, nor the world's law;
    The world affords no law to make thee rich;
    Then be not poor, but break it and take this.
Apothecary
    My poverty but not my will consents.   *75*
Romeo
    I pay thy poverty and not thy will.
Apothecary
    Put this in any liquid thing you will
    And drink it off; and if you had the strength
    Of twenty men, it would dispatch you straight.
Romeo
    There is thy gold—worse poison to men's souls,   *80*
    Doing more murder in this loathsome world
    Than these poor compounds that thou mayst not sell.

85. *cordial:* a comforting drink. It is comforting to Romeo because it will bring him the death he longs for.

SCENE II

5-12. In his agitation, Friar John gives a very confusing account of what has happened. It appears that he had gone to look for another Franciscan friar to go with him on his visit to Mantua. He eventually found his man visiting the sick in a house which was suspected of harbouring the plague; the health authorities, as the custom then was, shut them up in the house for fear of their spreading the infection. **6.** *to associate me:* to accompany me.

18. *nice:* trivial.
18-19. *full of charge Of dear import:* full of important news. The letter is, of course, one informing Romeo of Juliet's pretended death and instructing him to come to Verona to collect her when she awakens.

I sell thee poison: thou hast sold me none.
Farewell; buy food, and get thyself in flesh.
Come, cordial and not poison, go with me   85
To Juliet's grave; for there must I use thee.

Exeunt

SCENE II—*Friar Lawrence's cell*

Enter FRIAR JOHN

Friar John
  Holy Franciscan friar! Brother, ho!

Enter FRIAR LAWRENCE

Friar Lawrence
  This same should be the voice of Friar John.
  Welcome from Mantua! What says Romeo?
  Or, if his mind be writ, give me his letter.
Friar John
  Going to find a barefoot brother out,   5
  One of our order, to associate me,
  Here in this city visiting the sick,
  And finding him, the searchers of the town,
  Suspecting that we both were in a house
  Where the infectious pestilence did reign,   10
  Seal'd up the doors, and would not let us forth,
  So that my speed to Mantua there was stay'd.
Friar Lawrence
  Who bare my letter, then, to Romeo?
Friar John
  I could not send it—here it is again—
  Nor get a messenger to bring it thee,   15
  So fearful were they of infection.
Friar Lawrence
  Unhappy fortune! By my brotherhood,
  The letter was not nice, but full of charge
  Of dear import; and the neglecting it
  May do much danger. Friar John, go hence;   20

237

21. *iron crow:* crowbar.

26. *beshrew:* greatly blame.
27. *accidents:* occurrences, mischances.

SCENE III

Paris has come to lay flowers at Juliet's tomb and to watch over it during the night.

1-9. It is not clear why Paris is so anxious not to be seen.

12. *thy bridal bed:* this would have been the first night after their wedding.

Get me an iron crow, and bring it straight
Unto my cell.

Friar John

Brother, I'll go and bring it thee.

Exit

Friar Lawrence

Now must I to the monument alone.
Within this three hours will fair Juliet wake;   *25*
She will beshrew me much that Romeo
Hath had no notice of these accidents.
But I will write again to Mantua,
And keep her at my cell till Romeo come—
Poor living corse, clos'd in a dead man's tomb!   *30*

Exit

SCENE III—*Verona. A churchyard; in it the tomb of the Capulets*

Enter PARIS, *and his* PAGE *bearing flowers and a torch*

Paris

Give me thy torch, boy; hence, and stand aloof;
Yet put it out, for I would not be seen.
Under yond yew trees lay thee all along,
Holding thy ear close to the hollow ground;
So shall no foot upon the churchyard tread—   *5*
Being loose, unfirm, with digging up of graves—
But thou shalt hear it. Whistle then to me,
As signal that thou hear'st something approach.
Give me those flowers. Do as I bid thee, go.

Page [*Aside*]

I am almost afraid to stand alone   *10*
Here in the churchyard; yet I will adventure.

Retires

Paris

Sweet flower, with flowers thy bridal bed I strew—

239

13. *canopy:* an Elizabethan bed had a covering high over it, supported by posts at the corners. Since Juliet's *bridal bed* is in fact a tomb, she is covered over by the stone roof of the tomb.
14. He intends to sprinkle water on the tomb.
16. *obsequies:* the ceremony of mourning.

20. *To cross:* to hinder.

32. *dear employment:* important business.
33. *jealous:* suspicious.

O woe, thy canopy is dust and stones!—
Which with sweet water nightly I will dew;
Or, wanting that, with tears distill'd by moans.　　15
The obsequies that I for thee will keep,
Nightly shall be to strew thy grave and weep.

The PAGE *whistles*

The boy gives warning something doth approach.
What cursed foot wanders this way to-night
To cross my obsequies and true love's rite?　　20
What, with a torch! Muffle me, night, awhile.

Retires

Enter ROMEO *and* BALTHASAR, *with a torch, a
mattock, and a crow of iron*

Romeo
　　Give me that mattock and the wrenching iron.
　　Hold, take this letter; early in the morning
　　See thou deliver it to my lord and father.
　　Give me the light; upon thy life I charge thee,　　25
　　Whate'er thou hear'st or seest, stand all aloof
　　And do not interrupt me in my course.
　　Why I descend into this bed of death
　　Is partly to behold my lady's face,
　　But chiefly to take thence from her dead finger　　30
　　A precious ring—a ring that I must use
　　In dear employment; therefore hence, be gone.
　　But if thou, jealous, dost return to pry
　　In what I farther shall intend to do,
　　By heaven, I will tear thee joint by joint,　　35
　　And strew this hungry churchyard with thy limbs.
　　The time and my intents are savage-wild,
　　More fierce and more inexorable far
　　Than empty tigers or the roaring sea.
Balthasar
　　I will be gone, sir, and not trouble ye.

43-4. Balthasar is a loyal servant and, fearing Romeo's intentions, he resolves to stay hidden.

45. *maw:* stomach.
46. *the dearest morsel of the earth* is, of course, Juliet.

48. *in despite:* to spite you. The tomb, already gorged with Juliet's body, is to receive his corpse also, whether it wants it or not.

53. *apprehend:* arrest.

58-67. Romeo speaks gently to Paris for, meaning to kill himself shortly, he has no wish to quarrel. He also speaks as though very much the senior man (*gentle youth . . . youth*).

68. *conjuration:* There is some doubt as to what Shakespeare actually wrote here—the meaning presumably is that Paris is not going to be talked round.
69. *felon:* criminal.

Romeo

   So shalt thou show me friendship. Take thou that;
   Live and be prosperous; and farewell, good fellow.

Balthasar [Aside]

   For all this same, I'll hide me hereabout;
   His looks I fear, and his intents I doubt. [*Retires*]

Romeo

   Thou detestable maw, thou womb of death,   45
   Gorg'd with the dearest morsel of the earth,
   Thus I enforce thy rotten jaws to open,

             Breaking open the tomb

   And, in despite, I'll cram thee with more food.

Paris

   This is that banish'd haughty Montague
   That murder'd my love's cousin—with which grief   50
   It is supposed the fair creature died—
   And here is come to do some villainous shame
   To the dead bodies. I will apprehend him.
   Stop thy unhallow'd toil, vile Montague.
   Can vengeance be pursued further than death?   55
   Condemned villain, I do apprehend thee.
   Obey, and go with me; for thou must die.

Romeo

   I must indeed; and therefore came I hither.
   Good gentle youth, tempt not a desp'rate man;
   Fly hence, and leave me. Think upon these gone;   60
   Let them affright thee. I beseech thee, youth,
   Put not another sin upon my head
   By urging me to fury; O, be gone!
   By heaven, I love thee better than myself,
   For I come hither arm'd against myself.   65
   Stay not, be gone; live, and hereafter say
   A madman's mercy bid thee run away.

Paris

   I do defy thy conjuration,
   And apprehend thee for a felon here.

82. There is no sense of rivalry here; Romeo feels that Paris and he have been alike caught up in a web of fate.

84. *A lantern:* a room with a dome or other construction at the top, through which light can pass. Romeo is saying that Juliet's body is a source of light which turns the grave into a *lantern*, in this sense.

86. *a feasting presence:* a presence chamber prepared for a feast. A presence chamber is a palace-room in which a king or queen receives guests.

87. *Death:* Paris.
a dead man: Romeo—he is about to kill himself.

88-120. This is a wonderful speech which must be read aloud to catch the rhythms and cadences, which are so expressive in Romeo's lingering farewell to his apparently dead wife and his resignation to the fate that has shadowed him throughout the play.

90. *lightning:* we should spell the word 'lightening' today. It means an interval of light-heartedness.

91. Romeo gazes at his wife who lies seemingly dead in her wedding dress.

94. *ensign:* banner. Juliet's face still has the fresh colour of a living person, not the paleness of the dead. The image is of a battle between Beauty and Death.

omeo

Wilt thou provoke me? Then have at thee, boy! 70

They fight

age

O lord, they fight! I will go call the watch.

Exit. PARIS *falls*

aris

O, I am slain! If thou be merciful,
Open the tomb, lay me with Juliet. [*Dies*]

omeo

In faith, I will. Let me peruse this face.
Mercutio's kinsman, noble County Paris! 75
What said my man, when my betossed soul
Did not attend him as we rode? I think
He told me Paris should have married Juliet.
Said he not so, or did I dream it so?
Or am I mad, hearing him talk of Juliet, 80
To think it was so? O, give me thy hand,
One writ with me in sour misfortune's book!
I'll bury thee in a triumphant grave.
A grave? O no! A lantern, slaughter'd youth;
For here lies Juliet, and her beauty makes 85
This vault a feasting presence full of light.
Death, lie thou there, by a dead man interr'd.

Laying PARIS *in the tomb*

How oft when men are at the point of death
Have they been merry! Which their keepers call
A lightning before death. O, how may I 90
Call this a lightning? O my love! my wife!
Death, that hath suck'd the honey of thy breath,
Hath had no power yet upon thy beauty.
Thou art not conquer'd; beauty's ensign yet
Is crimson in thy lips and in thy cheeks, 95
And death's pale flag is not advanced there.

102-5. Wondering at Juliet's beauty, Romeo plays with the idea that Death has fallen in love with her body and is preserving it from decay in order that he may remain her lover.

105. *paramour:* mistress.

111. *the yoke of inauspicious stars:* 'the controlling influence of an unhappy fate.'

115. *A dateless bargain:* an eternal agreement.
engrossing: all-consuming.
116. *Come, bitter conduct:* he is now talking to the vial of poison which he is holding.
conduct: conductor.
117-18. Compare Act II, Scene ii, lines 82-4.
desperate pilot: himself.
thy sea-sick weary bark: his body, tired of life, is compared to a ship after a long voyage.

122. *Who's there?* A lantern, which the Friar is carrying, lights up Balthasar.

Tybalt, liest thou there in thy bloody sheet?
O, what more favour can I do to thee
Than with that hand that cut thy youth in twain
To sunder his that was thine enemy?   *100*
Forgive me, cousin. Ah, dear Juliet,
Why art thou yet so fair? Shall I believe
That unsubstantial Death is amorous,
And that the lean abhorred monster keeps
Thee here in dark to be his paramour?   *105*
For fear of that I still will stay with thee,
And never from this palace of dim night
Depart again. Here, here will I remain
With worms that are thy chambermaids. O, here
Will I set up my everlasting rest,   *110*
And shake the yoke of inauspicious stars
From this world-wearied flesh. Eyes, look your last.
Arms, take your last embrace. And, lips, O you
The doors of breath, seal with a righteous kiss
A dateless bargain to engrossing death!   *115*
Come, bitter conduct, come, unsavoury guide.
Thou desperate pilot, now at once run on
The dashing rocks thy sea-sick weary bark.
Here's to my love! [*Drinks*] O true apothecary!
Thy drugs are quick. Thus with a kiss I die. [*Falls*]   *120*

    Enter FRIAR LAWRENCE, *with lantern, crow, and*
                  spade

Friar Lawrence
  Saint Francis be my speed! How oft to-night
  Have my old feet stumbled at graves! Who's there?
Balthasar
  Here's one, a friend, and one that knows you well.
Friar Lawrence
  Bliss be upon you! Tell me, good my friend,
  What torch is yond that vainly lends his light   *125*
  To grubs and eyeless skulls? As I discern,
  It burneth in the Capels' monument.

144-7. Friar Lawrence's speech is very broken up, because he is movin
about the tomb, discovering who is there.

Balthasar
　It doth so, holy sir; and there's my master,
　One that you love.
Friar Lawrence　　　Who is it?
Balthasar　　　　　　　　Romeo.
Friar Lawrence
　How long hath he been there?
Balthasar　　　　　　　Full half an hour.　　*130*
Friar Lawrence
　Go with me to the vault.
Balthasar　　　　　　I dare not, sir.
　My master knows not but I am gone hence,
　And fearfully did menace me with death,
　If I did stay to look on his intents.
Friar Lawrence
　Stay, then, I'll go alone; fear comes upon me;　　*135*
　O, much I fear some ill unthrifty thing.
Balshasar
　As I did sleep under this yew tree here,
　I dreamt my master and another fought,
　And that my master slew him.
Friar Lawrence　　　　　Romeo!
　Alack, alack, what blood is this which stains　　*140*
　The stony entrance of this sepulchre?
　What mean these masterless and gory swords
　To lie discolour'd by this place of peace?

Enters the tomb

Romeo! O, pale! Who else? What, Paris too?
And steep'd in blood? Ah, what an unkind hour　　*145*
Is guilty of this lamentable chance!
The lady stirs.

JULIET *wakes*

Juliet
　O comfortable friar! Where is my lord?
　I do remember well where I should be,
　And there I am. Where is my Romeo?　　*150*

249

156-7. 'I will secure your entry into a convent.'

158. *the watch:* men who patrolled the streets at night.

163. *O churl!* She chides Romeo for being unkind in having drunk all the poison himself.

166. *a restorative:* death will restore them to one another.

Noise within

Friar Lawrence
    I hear some noise. Lady, come from that nest
    Of death, contagion, and unnatural sleep;
    A greater power than we can contradict
    Hath thwarted our intents. Come, come away;
    Thy husband in thy bosom there lies dead;   *155*
    And Paris too. Come, I'll dispose of thee
    Among a sisterhood of holy nuns.
    Stay not to question, for the watch is coming;
    Come, go, good Juliet. I dare no longer stay.
Juliet
    Go, get thee hence, for I will not away.   *160*

Exit FRIAR LAWRENCE

    What's here? A cup, clos'd in my true love's hand?
    Poison, I see, hath been his timeless end.
    O churl! drunk all, and left no friendly drop
    To help me after? I will kiss thy lips;
    Haply some poison yet doth hang on them,   *165*
    To make me die with a restorative.
    Thy lips are warm.

Kisses him

First Watch [*Within*]   Lead, boy. Which way?
Juliet
    Yea, noise? Then I'll be brief. O happy dagger!

Snatching Romeo's dagger

    This is thy sheath; there rust, and let me die.

She stabs herself and falls on Romeo's body

Enter WATCH, *with* PARIS'S PAGE

Page
    This is the place; there, where the torch doth burn.   *170*
First Watch
    The ground is bloody; search about the churchyard.

172. *attach:* arrest.

179. *true ground:* true cause—another pun with *ground* (earth) in line 178.
180. 'We cannot discover without further evidence.'

Go, some of you, whoe'er you find attach.

Exeunt some of the WATCH

Pitiful sight! here lies the County slain;
And Juliet bleeding, warm, and newly dead,
Who here hath lain this two days buried.   *175*
Go, tell the Prince; run to the Capulets;
Raise up the Montagues; some others search.

Exeunt others of the WATCH

We see the ground whereon these woes do lie;
But the true ground of all these piteous woes
We cannot without circumstance descry.   *180*

Re-enter some of the WATCH *with* BALTHASAR

Second Watch
   Here's Romeo's man; we found him in the churchyard.
First Watch
   Hold him in safety till the Prince come hither.

Re-enter FRIAR LAWRENCE *and another* WATCHMAN

Third Watch
   Here is a friar that trembles, sighs, and weeps;
   We took this mattock and this spade from him,
   As he was coming from this churchyard's side.   *185*
First Watch
   A great suspicion; stay the friar too.

Enter the PRINCE *and* ATTENDANTS

Prince
   What misadventure is so early up,
   That calls our person from our morning rest?

Enter CAPULET, LADY CAPULET, *and* OTHERS

Capulet
   What should it be that is so shriek'd abroad?
Lady Capulet
   The people in the street cry 'Romeo',   *190*

195. *Juliet, dead before:* the Watchman is puzzled; he saw Juliet dead and buried but now her body is still warm and apparently just killed from stabbing.

202-3. Capulet points to the empty sheath that Romeo is wearing.

206. 'That calls me to my grave.' Lady Capulet is, of course, not old (she is in fact twenty-eight).

Some 'Juliet' and some 'Paris'; and all run,
With open outcry, toward our monument.
Prince
What fear is this which startles in our ears?
First Watch
Sovereign, here lies the County Paris slain;
And Romeo dead; and Juliet, dead before,   *195*
Warm and new kill'd.
Prince
Search, seek, and know how this foul murder comes.
First Watch
Here is a friar, and slaughter'd Romeo's man,
With instruments upon them fit to open
These dead men's tombs.   *200*
Capulet
O heavens! O wife, look how our daughter bleeds!
This dagger hath mista'en, for, lo, his house
Is empty on the back of Montague,
And it mis-sheathed in my daughter's bosom.
Lady Capulet
O me! this sight of death is as a bell   *205*
That warns my old age to a sepulchre.

Enter MONTAGUE *and* OTHERS

Prince
Come, Montague, for thou art early up
To see thy son and heir more early down.
Montague
Alas, my liege, my wife is dead to-night;
Grief of my son's exile hath stopp'd her breath. *210*
What further woe conspires against mine age?
Prince
Look, and thou shalt see.
Montague
O thou untaught! what manners is in this,
To press before thy father to a grave?

255

218. 'I will lead you in your mourning.'

220. 'Bear these misfortunes patiently.'

222-4. This passage is confused; the Friar says that he is under the greatest suspicion, implicated both by the time and the place at which he was caught, but he is actually the least likely to have committed the crime.

225-6. 'Both to charge and condemn myself and at the same time to exonerate myself.'

228. *my short date of breath:* 'the short time I have to live.'

236. *You:* he turns to Capulet.

242. *tutor'd by my art:* 'taught by my knowledge of medicines.'

246. *as:* on.

Prince

  Seal up the mouth of outrage for a while,   *215*
  Till we can clear these ambiguities,
  And know their spring, their head, their true descent;
  And then will I be general of your woes,
  And lead you even to death. Meantime forbear,
  And let mischance be slave to patience.   *220*
  Bring forth the parties of suspicion.

Friar Lawrence

  I am the greatest, able to do least,
  Yet most suspected, as the time and place
  Doth make against me, of this direful murder;
  And here I stand, both to impeach and purge   *225*
  Myself condemned and myself excus'd.

Prince

  Then say at once what thou dost know in this.

Friar Lawrence

  I will be brief, for my short date of breath
  Is not so long as is a tedious tale.
  Romeo, there dead, was husband to that Juliet;   *230*
  And she, there dead, that Romeo's faithful wife.
  I married them; and their stol'n marriage-day
  Was Tybalt's doomsday, whose untimely death
  Banish'd the new-made bridegroom from this city;
  For whom, and not for Tybalt, Juliet pin'd.   *235*
  You, to remove that siege of grief from her,
  Betroth'd, and would have married her perforce,
  To County Paris. Then comes she to me,
  And with wild looks bid me devise some mean
  To rid her from this second marriage,   *240*
  Or in my cell there would she kill herself.
  Then gave I her, so tutor'd by my art,
  A sleeping potion; which so took effect
  As I intended, for it wrought on her
  The form of death. Meantime I writ to Romeo   *245*
  That he should hither come as this dire night
  To help to take her from her borrow'd grave,

264-5. *and to the marriage Her nurse is privy.* 'Her Nurse knows all about the marriage.'

269. *still:* always. The Friar's long speech, which may seem unnecessary to a modern audience, is, in fact, needed to prepare the way for the parents' reconciliation, which is the conclusion of the play and an essential part of Shakespeare's scheme. See Prologue to Act I, Scene i, line 11.

Being the time the potion's force should cease.
But he which bore my letter, Friar John,
Was stay'd by accident, and yesternight   250
Return'd my letter back. Then all alone
At the prefixed hour of her waking
Came I to take her from her kindred's vault;
Meaning to keep her closely at my cell
Till I conveniently could send to Romeo.   255
But when I came, some minute ere the time
Of her awakening, here untimely lay
The noble Paris and true Romeo dead.
She wakes; and I entreated her come forth,
And bear this work of heaven with patience.   260
But then a noise did scare me from the tomb,
And she, too desperate, would not go with me,
But, as it seems, did violence on herself.
All this I know, and to the marriage
Her nurse is privy; and if ought in this   265
Miscarried by my fault, let my old life
Be sacrific'd, some hour before his time,
Unto the rigour of severest law.

Prince

We still have known thee for a holy man.
Where's Romeo's man? What can he say to this?   270

Balthasar

I brought my master news of Juliet's death;
And then in post he came from Mantua
To this same place, to this same monument.
This letter he early bid me give his father;
And threaten'd me with death, going in the vault, 275
If I departed not and left him there.

Prince

Give me the letter, I will look on it.
Where is the County's page that rais'd the watch?
Sirrah, what made your master in this place?

Page

He came with flowers to strew his lady's grave;   280

292. 'That fate finds a way to kill your children through their love for each other.'

293. *winking at:* 'shutting my eyes to.'

294. *brace:* two, i.e., Paris and Mercutio.

296-7. Montague's hand in reconciliation is all that Capulet, as Juliet's father, requires as a marriage gift (*jointure*) from the bridegroom's father.

And bid me stand aloof, and so I did.
Anon comes one with light to ope the tomb;
And by and by my master drew on him;
And then I ran away to call the watch.

Prince

This letter doth make good the friar's words,   *285*
Their course of love, the tidings of her death;
And here he writes that he did buy a poison
Of a poor pothecary, and therewithal
Came to this vault to die, and lie with Juliet.
Where be these enemies? Capulet, Montague,   *290*
See what a scourge is laid upon your hate,
That heaven finds means to kill your joys with love!
And I, for winking at your discords too,
Have lost a brace of kinsmen. All are punish'd.

Capulet

O brother Montague, give me thy hand.   *295*
This is my daughter's jointure, for no more
Can I demand.

Montague   But I can give thee more;
For I will raise her statue in pure gold,
That whiles Verona by that name is known,
There shall no figure at such rate be set   *300*
As that of true and faithful Juliet.

Capulet

As rich shall Romeo's by his lady's lie—
Poor sacrifices of our enmity!

Prince

A glooming peace this morning with it brings;
The sun for sorrow will not show his head.   *305*
Go hence, to have more talk of these sad things;
Some shall be pardon'd and some punished;
For never was a story of more woe
Than this of Juliet and her Romeo.

Exeunt

SUMMING UP

It was mentioned in the Introduction that the action of the play is simple and compressed, although holding a great variety of material, and this observation is borne out by our knowledge of the time scheme, which is very tightly constructed. The entire movement is completed in six days. I may also be clear now that *Romeo and Juliet* is not primarily a tragedy which arises from the characteristics of the two lovers, but that it is rather the working out of the process of Fate.

It so happens that the Montagues and Capulets are quarrelling – we are not aware of the cause – and that Romeo and Juliet are born into this feud. It also so happens that Romeo falls in love with a Capulet, and then gets involved in the killing of Tybalt against his will, which brings about the Prince's sentence of banishment. Romeo's exile coincides with Capulet's decision to marry Juliet to Paris, and this leads to Friar Lawrence's attempt to help, which fails when Friar John is unable to deliver the letter. When we see, in addition to the social environment of Verona, the nature of Romeo and Juliet's passion, we understand that the combination of those people and those circumstances could not result in a different ending.

It is often misleading to think about Shakespeare's plays simply in terms of characters. In *Romeo and Juliet* for example, the social conditions in Verona, the plot, and the language of the play are each just as important as characterization. Nevertheless the play obviously does include a number of characters so vividly put before us that we are bound to be interested in them as persons, as well as in their contribution to the working out of the plot of the play.

Capulet, Juliet's father, is wealthy and well into middle age; he likes to pose as an indulgent father – witness his conversation with Paris when the young man first asks about marrying Juliet – and as the benevolent head of an important family in Verona. He can be heartily good humoured when everything is going his way but when he does not get his own way, he quickly appears as an overbearing brute. The language he uses to his young daughter is unforgivably insulting – even the Nurse and Lady Capulet protest – and shows the essential coarseness of a man who is insensitive to any feelings but his own. He contributes more than anyone else to the tragic story of his daughter, but is quite unaware of what he is doing.

His wife is by comparison only slightly drawn for us: much younger (she is, we gather, only twenty-eight), she seems to be a cold unsympathetic woman; her principal part in the play is to make more pitiful the isolation of Juliet, when even her mother refuses sympathy.

The Nurse, the other prominent figure of the household to which Juliet belongs, is, by common consent, one of the most real and living of all the characters Shakespeare created. She is talkative – nothing can stop her rattling on; she quickly loses the point of what she is saying in a flood of detail. She is full of vitality, has a simple sense of humour and, most evidently, she has a coarse mind. Her thoughts turn with the slightest provocation, or with none, to sex, and to sex in the most earthy way. It is in this that her part in the play is most evidently seen, providing a most effective contrast to the purity and idealism of Juliet.

Of all the characters in the play, it is Juliet who develops and matures most remarkably. We first see her as a child-like and obedient young girl, with little experience of personal relationships beyond her family attachments, and apparently submissive to her mother's arrangement of the marriage with Paris:

> I'll look to like, if looking liking move;
> But no more deep will I endart mine eye
> Than your consent gives strength to make it fly

However, her love for Romeo quite transforms her character; we see her awakened into womanhood, and learning a set of personal values which rise above Verona's accepted social conventions. Her new-found maturity is revealed in the scene at her bedroom window when she expresses her complete faith in and love for Romeo. This development in her character is again exhibited in her unembarrassed attitude to sexuality. We must appreciate that she is a young girl and that this is her first and only love-affair and yet despite her inexperience she quickly forms an adult attitude to sex. She recognizes but does not distort its great importance in their relationship. The growth in her character also reveals her great courage and determination. She does not yield to Capulet's disgracefully violent abuse and she completely ignores the Nurse's suggestion that she should marry Paris to get out of her difficulties. Alone in her bedroom, she dares to take the Friar's potion and when she awakens in the tomb to find her lover dead, there is no hesitation in her resolve,

> *Yea, noise? Then I'll be brief. O happy dagger!*
> *This is thy sheath; there rust, and let me die*

The development of Romeo throughout the play complements that of Juliet; however, we may feel that he does not grow up as remarkably as she does. When we first see him, he is entangled in his affair with Rosaline; however, it must be made clear that this experience is very different from the passion he will later feel for Juliet. It was conventional in Elizabethan times for young men to sigh after, and write poetry to, hard-hearted ladies, and suffer when rejected. These were not so much authentic love-affairs as a sort of social affectation: the pretence of love and the posing as a desolate lover were all a kind of game. Romeo's relationship with Rosaline takes this form in the play. His advances are not returned by her and his infatuation seems to be a sickness, an affliction:

> *She hath forsworn to love, and in that vow*
> *Do I live dead that live to tell it now.*

We may initially feel with the Friar that Romeo's new love for Juliet is too impetuous to be really important, but are soon convinced of his seriousness, as Friar Lawrence is too. He is greatly involved with Juliet during the middle acts of the play, but we still see him jesting with his friends and getting caught up in a fatal sword-fight, which he has recognized as foolhardy. His futile revenge is to cost the lovers their lives. It is when we see his sheer hysteria after the news of his banishment that we realize that his involvement with Juliet has become total. Romeo does not achieve Juliet's stature until the final scenes of the play, when he cries.

Then I defy you, stars.

and accepts death to be with his love. He shows in that last fine soliloquy that he will cling to what was best in his human experience; the lovers have found a sublime unity.

Friar Lawrence as a character in the play is more important for what he does than for what he is. He marries the young lovers in haste, so making it necessary for Juliet to defy her father when he arranges the wedding with Paris. The Friar then provides her with the means, the sleeping potion, by which she may hope to escape from her impossible situation, and it is his arrangements which break down when the letter fails to reach Romeo, an incident which leads directly to Romeo's suicide. He is old, gentle and sympathetic as is fitting to his vocation, but rather alarmed by the rashness and impetuosity of young lovers. He sees the harm done by the family quarrel between Capulets and Montagues, and hopes that the marriage might be a means of healing it. That is all we know about him: but it is sufficient for the purpose of the play.

Tybalt is the kind of man the Elizabethans would have recognized at once: proud and quick-tempered, and concerned to be up with the latest trends in manner and in speech. Although he is supposed to be an Italian, Shakespeare, his English creator, presents him in such a way as to show through the comments of Mercutio the prejudices of some Englishmen, then and now, against their compatriots who copy foreign continental habits. Tybalt's particular enthusiasm is fencing, which he practises after the manner of the French, his conversation larded with a full range of technical terms. He is an exhibitionist, a 'show-off', *the courageous captain of compliments.* As with his uncle Capulet, his character is aptly fitted to the contribution he makes to the plot: it is his showiness that goads Mercutio into the duel which leads to Romeo's banishment.

Mercutio, like the Nurse, is more interesting for what he is than for what he does. His single important contribution to the action of the play is his challenge to Tybalt, which leads to his death and so to Romeo's banishment. But during that part of the play in which he is on the stage there is vivacity, a gaiety and high-spiritedness, which disappears with him. He is the principal exponent of the kind of word-play which was discussed in the Introduction, and when this provokes Romeo into retorting in the same way as in Act 2, Scene iv, the result is a dazzling display of verbal fireworks. It is he, too, who is the source of most of the outrageous sexual humour in *Romeo and Juliet*, particularly in baiting Romeo about his love-sickness for Rosaline. It is in this matter too that he has another dramatic function to perform: to Mercutio, who has never been touched by love, sex is a subject for humour, and Shakespeare makes very clear to us the contrast between him and Romeo by giving as a prologue to the love duet at Juliet's window a scene in which Mercutio's bawdy is at its broadest. Romeo, on Shakespeare's stage, listens to this unseen, and he dismisses it in a line –

He jests at scars that never felt a wound.

Shakespeare's judgement was wholly sound in removing him at a particular point: the tragic course of events in the second half of the play could have no place for the impudent gaiety of a Mercutio, and in the light of the elevated passion of the two lovers his attitude to sexuality would have seemed discordant, perhaps even silly. In this respect, his character is deficient, but on the other hand one loves him for all that he is, for being a man who even at death has a pun on his lips:

Ask for me tomorrow, and you shall find me a grave man.

No consideration of *Romeo and Juliet* should neglect to give proper consideration to the fact that what made it possible for Shakespeare to raise a familiar and ordinary Italian short story to the level of a splendid play was his command of language.

An examination of two of Capulet's speeches will give some idea of how the man's character and moods are created for us through the phrases and rhythms that he uses (Act I, Scene v, lines 14-31). Here Capulet is jocular, being familiar with the young ladies and exchanging sentimental memories with his contemporaries. Notice how these first characteristics are given expression through the choice of words and the quick movement of the sounds in *am I come near ye now*? and *give room*; *and foot it girls*. For the expression of the other mood, Shakespeare employs a long, falling rhythm: *For you and I are past our dancing days* and *'Tis gone, 'tis gone, 'tis gone!*

In another scene (Act III, Scene v, lines 151-157), we see Capulet in an abusive and bullying mood; here, the repeated alliteration seems to make the words spit out and the brutality of the expression indicates the coarseness of the man. The phrase, *But fettle your fine joints 'gainst Thursday next*, sounds as if he is treating his daughter as an animal. When he is even angrier, the rhythm is made to break down altogether, and only short wild words can explode from Capulet's mouth (line 193).

In complete contrast to this, we can see how Shakespeare organizes language to create the sententious, moralizing character of Friar Lawrence (Act II, Scene iii, lines 1-30; Act III Scene iii, lines 108-158). Here Shakespeare employs elaborate sentences, giving himself time for the full development of similes and metaphors, and in the second speech, carrying an involved but logical argument through to its conclusion.

When we turn from the Friar to the poetry of Juliet's speech, we see Shakespeare controlling the language to create an urgent yet gentle appeal in Act III, Scene ii, lines 17-25. The repeated words, *come, night, Romeo* express Juliet's longing to be with her lover and yet the beauty of the picture of snow upon a raven's back, and the quality of freshness of the words *new snow* maintain the serenity of the mood. Notice how in both instances the three short phrases are followed by images with an extended slow, flowing rhythm. Both the strength of her desire and the tenderness of her feelings are captured in the varying sounds.

If we turn to one of the finest passages of poetry in the play, that is, Romeo's last soliloquy (Act V, Scene ii, lines 106-120), we see how Shakespeare uses images and rhythms to make us understand that to Romeo death is welcome and to appreciate that what is happening is inevitable. Juliet's tomb is for Romeo a *palace* and within the terms of the image even the worms which will eat their bodies are made less repulsive by being visualized as their *chambermaids*. What he is going to is *everlasting rest* – the phrase itself is suggestive of complete and final release. The word *yoke* sums up the way Fate (the *inauspicious stars*) has controlled his life. And the long rhythms of the whole sentence suggest a movement to a full close, like the recognizably final cadence of a piece of music.

THEME INDEX

The 'Generation Gap'

Romeo and Juliet are driven to behave as they do because they know that there is no possibility of their feelings being understood by their parents. *O Romeo, Romeo!* cries Juliet, when she discovers the identity of her lover, *wherefore art thou Romeo? Deny thy father and refuse thy name;* (II ii 33-36). Juliet in particular suffers under an insensitive mother and an abusive father (III v 139-204). The Nurse, too, another of the older generation, although apparently unusually sympathetic, abandons Juliet when she most needs help; *O most wicked fiend!* Juliet calls her (III v 205-end).

The Family Feud

Their parents' attitudes towards the love of Romeo and Juliet are partly conditioned by the Capulet-Montague feud. Long-standing hatred between families still exist in some Mediterranean countries, although the idea is strange to most of us. It is certainly destructive of the love of the two young people, who themselves have little feeling for it. The situation is made clear in the sonnet spoken before the start of the play proper: *Two households, both alike in dignity,* says Chorus, *From ancient grudge break to new mutiny.* He speaks of *the continuance of their parents' rage, Which, but their children's end, nought could remove.* The theme is continued as soon as Sampson and Gregory appear, and dominates the first scene. (See also: I v 58-62; II ii 60-65; III i; V iii 290-303.)

Fate

It is through the family feud that Fate principally operates in the play. *A pair of star-cross'd lovers* (Prologue, Act I, line 6): these are the words in which Shakespeare introduces Romeo and Juliet to us. We know from the first that there is to be no 'living happily ever after' for these two: they are destined to die. A boy and a girl are born into families

269

which make it impossible that a marriage between them could be acceptable. They meet, very improbably, and fall in love at first sight (I v 42-51 and 130-139). Within hours of a secret marriage, Romeo reluctantly fights Tybalt after a chance meeting in the streets, kills him and is banished (III i). On the very same day Juliet learns that she is to be forced into marriage with another man (III v 107-196). The messenger taking news of Friar Lawrence's scheme never reaches Romeo (V ii 5-20), and the timing of the events which close the play is such that Romeo kills himself before Juliet awakes, and Juliet kills herself before the Watch arrives, though all these events take place within a few minutes of one another (V ii and iii). In addition we may feel that Fate is operating at deeper and less expressible levels: is it possible for us to conceive of a love so wholly absorbing, so passionate, so idealized, being able to survive in the world as it is? (See V iii 110-112).

Love

Three aspects of sexual love are illustrated in *Romeo and Juliet*. First, the 'calf-love' of Romeo for Rosaline, which is little more than affectation (I i 195-end; I ii 45-end; I iv 14-39). Second, Paris's love for Juliet. This is deeper, but wholly proper and conventional: Paris makes an approach to Juliet's father first, and refers to her always with great respect (III iv; IV i 1-43; V iii 1-73). Third, the overwhelming passion of Romeo and Juliet which is conveyed most vividly and movingly (II ii, III ii, III v 1-36 and V iii 22-169).

Bawdy

There is a very different aspect of sex in the play—the bawdiness freely expressed by Mercutio, the Nurse and other characters. There is probably more humorous talk about sex in *Romeo and Juliet* than in any other play of Shakespeare's. The bawdy is there for two main reasons: because it amused the audience (I i 1-32; II i 17-end) and because it enables a most significant contrast to be made between the gay flippancy of Mercutio's attitude to sex (together with the comic vulgarity of the Nurse's remarks) and the seriousness and beauty of the love of Romeo and Juliet.

Imagery

In *Romeo and Juliet* Shakespeare's style varies between a rather self-conscious use of words and devices (characteristic of his early work) and a much more profound employment of all the resources of language. The imagery of the play reflects this dual effect. At I iii 82-93 Lady Capulet compares Paris's face with a book, and elaborates the idea lengthily in a purely descriptive way. There are other examples of the same kind of imagery at II iii 9-12 and III v 197-8 and particularly in the speeches of Romeo before his whole life is changed by meeting Juliet: I i 184-188, I iv 19-22, etc. Elaboration sometimes achieves a deeper meaning, in reflecting the character of the speaker: e.g. the pompous Capulet makes detailed comparisons with his weeping daughter (III v 129-137) in a manner that is typical of him. In the second half of the play the imagery has a much more pervasive effect. When Juliet is waiting for Romeo at the beginning of III ii, she speaks elaborately of the night, but the elaborateness now stresses that the lovers look on the night as the positive and benevolent background for their love: the imagery is both witty and passionate.

But the most striking use of imagery lies at the heart of the play's development. When the lovers meet for the first time, at Capulet's house, they address each other in a beautifully artificial way, with plenty of wit but little passion (I v 91-108). In the garden scene and the balcony scene, however, everything is changed and intensified, and the imagery reflects this: II ii 26-32, 107-124, 158-167; III v 1-11, 17-36, etc.

The dominant feature of the play's imagery is the contrast between light and darkness, and the most remarkable aspect of this is the way in which Romeo and Juliet appear to each other as luminous objects in surrounding darkness (II ii 15-22; III ii 17-19 and 21-25; V iii 85-86). The emotional and dramatic effects of this are obvious.

FURTHER READING

An invaluable essay is Harley Granville-Barker's 'Preface' to the play in Vol. 2 of *Preface to Shakespeare* (Batsford). Also useful is *Twentieth Century Interpretations of Romeo and Juliet* (Prentice Hall) edited by Douglas Cole. Available as a paperback (Spectrum Book series), it contains *Shakespeare's Experimental Tragedy* by H. B. Charlton, *Shakespeare's Young Lovers* by Elmer Stoll, *Romeo and Juliet* by W. H. Clemen, *Form and Formality in 'Romeo and Juliet'* by Harry Levin, *Light images in 'Romeo and Juliet'* by Caroline Spurgeon, as well as briefer 'points of view' about the play from, among others, J. Dover Wilson, T. S. Eliot, Franklin Dickey and Nevill Coghill.